PIANO BY HEART COMPANION

ADVANCED PIANO MEMORIZATION EXERCISES

◆ ◆ ◆

by
BERNARD M. PATTEN,
AB, SUMMA CUM LAUDE, COLUMBIA COLLEGE
MD, COLLEGE OF PHYSICIANS AND SURGEONS, COLUMBIA UNIVERSITY

Fellow of the America College of Physicians

Fellow of the Royal Society of Medicine

Fellow of the Texas Neurological Society

Fellow of the American Academy of Neurology

Memory Fellow of the New York Academy of Medicine

Diplomate of the American Board of Psychiatry and Neurology

Formerly Instructor in Neuroscience, Philosophy and Mental Gymnastics
at Rice University, School of Continuing Studies, Houston, TX

PIANO BY HEART COMPANION

ADVANCED PIANO MEMORIZATION EXERCISES

Copyright © 2025 Bernard Michael Patten, M.D.

All rights reserved. No part of this publication may be reproduced, distributed, or transmitted in any form or by any means, including photocopying, recording, or other electronic or mechanical methods, without the prior written permission of the publisher, except in the case of brief quotations embodied in critical reviews and certain other noncommercial uses permitted by copyright law. Any perceived slight against any individual is purely unintentional.

For permission requests, write to the publisher at:
contact@identitypublications.com.

Ordering Information:
Quantity sales. Special discounts are available on quantity purchases by corporations, associations, and others. For details, contact the publisher at the address above.

Orders by U.S. trade bookstores and wholesalers.
Please contact Identity Publications:
Tel: (805) 259-3724 or visit www.IdentityPublications.com.

ISBN-13: 979-8-3485-0557-8 (ebook)
ISBN-13: 979-8-3485-0556-1 (paperback)
ISBN-13: 979-8-3485-1124-1 (hardcover)

First Edition
Publishing by Identity Publications
www.IdentityPublications.com

CONTENTS

❖❖❖

Preface. iv
Anacrusis. 1
Legato 3
Upbeat. 4
Crescendo 8
About Für Elise. 22
How to Do an Analysis of *Für Elise* *26*
The Marriage of Two Minds: Conscious and
Unconscious 29
How to Employ Multimodalities 32
Approaching the Hard Parts with Equanimity 42
Headed into the Homestretch 47
The Visual Modality 54
Intellectual. 57
Dr. Patten's Intellectual Analysis of *Für Elise* *60*
Program Music 70
Welcome back from your break!. 79
Review Time Is Never Wasted 85
The Profound Advantage of Pattern Recognition. . . . 91
Attacking C by Divide and Conquer. 96
Whence Comes the Charm of Music? 107
Memorizing Music Is Hard Work 113
Style and Interpretation. 116
Putting It All Together 120
Bibliography 122

PREFACE

◆ ◆ ◆

Welcome to the short companion volume for *Piano by Heart*. Here, you will find more advanced exercises that challenge you with the memory principles I introduced in that book. If, for some reason, you haven't already, I highly suggest you put this book down until you've had a chance to read through that one thoroughly. Then, see if you're ready to test your memory and piano chops with what follows!

BERNARD M. PATTEN

ANACRUSIS

❖❖❖

Forewarned is Forearmed

Before you start your memory work, I want to warn you about what to expect. That warning may help you understand yourself and the human condition better, and it may better equip you to deal with the usual situations that confront the average pianist.

General Advice: Don't Give Yourself Excuses Not to Memorize

Rule #1: Be alone. Otherwise, someone near will give you an excuse not to apply yourself to the task. That means no telephone, no idle chatter, and no thinking about chores that need to be done—they can wait. There should be no demands made on you by children, spouses, or partners. Talk with them, explain that you need private time to memorize music. Usually, they will understand. People are easy to manage. The real problems will come from inside yourself. Managing yourself can be the challenge.

When you actually sit down to memorize, what is the first thing that will happen? Here's the prediction:

Resistance, that's what.

You will (from personal experience, I predict) be seized with an incredible urge to sharpen your pencils, clean your room, or feed the cats. You'll invent reasons or excuses not to memorize.

PIANO BY HEART COMPANION

Writers have the same problem with resistance. Ernest Hemingway sharpened dozens of pencils before he wrote. Willa Cather read the Bible before writing each day. And here's a story for you: John Donne tells us he liked to lie in an open coffin before picking up his pen.

Memorizing music is a real skill, like learning to fly an airplane or swim. You must make up your mind to work at it to master it, and you must do the work. So, when you sit down to memorize a piece, resist that sudden urge to clean the refrigerator, check your stock prices, wash the car, take a drive, watch TV, take a yoga class, or buy clothes or tools you don't need or want. You may suddenly feel angry at someone or something—or at nothing in particular. Recognize all these for what they are—mental mechanisms designed to make your brain avoid working on the memory task.

My major distraction when I sit down to memorize something is that I suddenly get the idea I should be memorizing something else, some other piece. That happened just today. I sat to memorize *Edelweiss* for a YouTube video and suddenly got in my head the idea to memorize *America the Beautiful*. I filed the idea of doing a different piece and focused on the task at hand. I'll come back to *America the Beautiful* sometime—maybe next week, maybe next month, maybe next year, maybe never.

You will have your own individual distractions. For me, distractions often concern ideas for other books. How about a book to help people lose weight? Title: *The Keep Your Mouth Shut Diet*, followed by *The Keep Your Mouth Shut Guide to a Happy Marriage*. Great titles, right? I'll file those potential books away. Many people could benefit from keeping their mouths shut, especially a current presidential candidate. Oh! That's it, another idea: *The Keep Your Mouth Shut Guide to Running for President*.

LEGATO

❖❖❖

Fight distractions with all your might. Start to memorize. Once you get the first few measures done, the distractions will diminish and may even disappear, and then the fun of new learning will keep you going (I hope). Take it easy. Memorize a little at a time. Repeat the few measures memorized right away and then repeat them at various time intervals. Pat yourself on the back when you get things right and keep working.

Repetition is the Key to Memory

Remember, repetition is the key to memorizing anything. Enjoy repetition and do it often at intervals and whenever you can. Check your work with the sheet music. Correct errors and play on. Look for patterns that can serve as a scaffold onto which you can hang some memory items. If you can't detect a pattern, make one up. With popular songs, use the lyrics as the scaffold. That works for me and it might work for you.

UPBEAT

◆ ◆ ◆

Let's start with *When the Saints Go Marching In*. Looking over the sheet from *The American Song Treasury*, here's my take:

1. Tempo is not too fast and with a bouncy spirit.
2. Key looks like D major and not B minor. The last measure confirms this by ending in the root note D in the treble and bass. So, I expect D major, some A major, and some G major (I, V, and IV).
3. Looks like four quarter notes to the measure.
4. There are 17 measures, 15 of which look unique by eyeball.
5. The lyrics are easy to remember, and I was able to recite them after two minutes. I had to be careful of the "Oh" that starts things. It's "Oh When" to start, and it doesn't start with "When" as I had previously thought. Also, it is "when the saints go marching in" and not "come marching in."
6. Applying Fermi estimation, it looks like two hours minimum to memorize and play correctly twice and four hours max. This makes 2 x 4 = 8, and the square root of 8 is 2.83. Therefore, the Fermi estimation is 2 hours and 50 minutes.
7. Applying Patten estimation, it looks like 15 unique measures and a note density of about 6.5 by eyeball estimation. But as an exercise, I counted all the notes in the measures. There are 17 measures and a total of 113 notes for an average note density of 6.65. Therefore, the Patten estimation is 30 x 6.65 = 199 minutes or about 3.5 hours.

Next, I'll look up the history of the piece and get some idea of the way it was traditionally played. I have a good idea of this because I've heard it played several times in New Orleans at the Heritage House.

(By the way, I resisted the temptation to consult artificial intelligence, although it would have had lots of interesting and probably dry, boring, and emotionless facts to relate and probably would have contributed to my general knowledge of the song. AI can be a teaching tool and a learning tool. Use it when you are in the mood. Right now, I'm not in the mood. I want to do my own research.)

Here's what I came up with:

When the Saints Go Marching In came into existence toward the end of the 19th century as a Negro spiritual. Most of the gospel songs were played quite sedately, but *Saints* was often an exception. The Holy Rollers, a religious sect given to high-keyed revival meetings, probably started the tradition of starting slow and soft and gradually playing faster and louder as chorus after chorus eventually became a frenzy of excitement. I have heard *Saints* played that way in New Orleans. I've seen movies of funeral parades in that fair city in which the first line (relatives and friends of the deceased) walks slowly and deliberately, fairly restrained and quiet, to the burial. After interment, the second line (mainly young hangers-on) goes wild and plays on the march back to the city center. Much of the latter music is polyphonic, with multiple players riffing their own ideas and versions, playing as their mood dictates, which was generally free, gay, and ad-lib. They shout, high step, strut, and shake everything they have on the way back. *Saints* was always the most-played song in the parade of non-legitimate mourners. This song is now one of the best-known jazz numbers in America. It was the virtual theme song of Louis Armstrong, who took it all over the United States and to Europe, Africa, and Russia.

PIANO BY HEART COMPANION

Analysis

Memorizing music is not easy, and this piece is no exception. It has four lines, and I decided to use that as part of my memory frame. Line one, measure one, is D F#, followed by what could be imagined as the completed trichord made by EF#G. Ugh! Too much work. I decided I needed to find an easier, more direct version. This version is too much work with too little reward. And it doesn't give me a musical chill.

So, I switch strategies. What to do? That is the question.

My wife's grandfather was a sergeant in World War I. He had an interesting handbook for sergeants. The handbook was like a catechism. It asked questions and then gave answers. One question relevant to his situation was, "What do you do if you don't know what to do?" I can just picture the men of the platoon, in some rain-drenched ditch, hovered over grandfather Hugh as he thumbs through the handbook looking for the answer to the above situation. The answer was, "Analyze the situation and act accordingly."

I will now apply that solution to my *Saints* problem.

Musicnotes.com has six versions of *Saints*, all available for download at a price. One version is the D major that I already worked on from *The American Song Treasury* and didn't like. Each Musicnotes.com version has a button to click so you can hear what they sound like. None of them pleases me. Sheetmusic.com has only one lead sheet of *Saints*, and I don't like it either because it sounds too simple.

On to YouTube.

Lots there, but nothing quite hits what I think it should sound like. But there was a simple page that just had letters, looking like this:

CEFG CEFG
CEFG EEDC
EGGG FEFG
ECDC

This code corresponds to the words I memorized, and I now get the idea that I can improvise my own version in a jiffy by fitting the keys to the rhythms I'm familiar with. CEFG = "Oh when the saints." Playing this on the piano sounds good. The next CEFG = "go marching in." No problem memorizing that sequence in less than two minutes. It is just C followed by the trichord EFG. I decide to be creative and structure my playing as answer and response between treble and bass, while imagining the bass as the chorus. So, I play CEFG in treble and then play the same in bass and repeat the same by playing CEFG in treble and then play the same in bass. I am not saying words but I am thinking them, and the narration helps my playing and recall. You can do the same if you wish. It's fun.

Next, I'm going to have more fun by playing the next chords after the F as CFAx2 in the bass. So far, I've spent 12 minutes actually working on the note sequence. Hot dog!

Then I slow down for the final ECDC and play E in treble and C major in bass, followed by C in treble and C major in bass, and then D followed by G7 or even just FG in bass, and finally C with FG followed by CFAx2 and end with C major in bass. This version pleases me, and I feel a sense of accomplishment in putting my own spin on this masterpiece of American Jazz.

CRESCENDO

♦ ♦ ♦

After reviewing and experimenting with different approaches, I made a video with three stanzas and uploaded it onto my YouTube Channel entitled *Bernard Patten*. Within two minutes of upload, there were 29 views and a nice compliment from Japan.

Next

Let's work on Chopin's *Prelude in A Major*. This is a classic and we won't have much leeway to change or rearrange it. But such is life.

Chopin Prelude in A Major

This is listed as Opus 28, No. 7. The significance of this listing will become clear as we look at the history of the piece. Remember, first we think about the piece and look it over before we actually sit at the piano and try to play. We ask ourselves questions so that we can become more comfortable about playing the masterpiece correctly. Also, we play it from notes and decide whether it is worth our time and effort to memorize the piece. The score is your reference. Consult it to verify your playing from memory.

Play the piece from notes to get a good foundation for your memory task. As you practice, think. Try to find what parts are easy and what parts are hard so you will be prepared to get this into memory. If you're unsure of your technique, rhythm, or pacing, ask your teacher for feedback.

Develop an Emotional Response to the Piece

You'll do better with the piece if you relate to it on an emotional level. Do you like it? Picture yourself bowing before an appreciative audience after performing it. Develop a meaningful relationship. In all human activity and affairs, relationships count. Reciting poetry you understand is far easier and more effective than reciting nonsense. Music can have meanings that you must develop for yourself. Meaning aids memory.

Look for patterns and images that may help convert difficult-to-recall items into easy-to-recall music. Asking yourself questions is often key to understanding. Some of your questions might include:

1. Tempo. Andantino. As I didn't know exactly what was meant by that tempo, I looked up the definition. Results: Lots of confusion among the definitions offered on the internet. The one I liked best was "faster than andante or slower than andante." That definition gives flexibility in deciding what's best. From the Polish professors on YouTube, I found that no one knows what tempo Chopin meant for this piece. All agree it is either faster or slower than andante. Chopin wrote "p dolce," so he probably wants us to play sweetly and softly, and probably not fast.
2. Key. A major. No question about that, as it states the key in the title. Because it is A major, we expect some E and some D, as E is the V note and D is IV. As long as we are at key, it's a good idea to memorize the exact reference label of the piece. Do this in case someone in your audience asks. Reply: *Chopin Opus 28, No. 7, Prelude in A Major*. Say this out loud

several times so you are used to hearing yourself say it. When directly addressing the audience, look directly at them, not the microphone or anything else. I usually make direct eye contact with one audience member who looks sympathetic. And for heaven's sake—smile! Audiences want to see happy people. Also, many scientific studies show that the more you smile, the happier you get. The brain takes the clue from the position of the facial muscles and assumes that if you are smiling, you must be happy.
3. Time. ¾, indicating three beats to the measure and each beat is a quarter note in value. Attention! Some beat ones are unique in that the beat consists of two items—one with a time value three times that of the other item. This is or can be a nice memory hook. To make it a memory hook, you must think about it and try to imagine how it might help your memory. Ask yourself if the 3-to-1 ratio occurs regularly, and if it does, it could become a memory tool.
4. Number of measures. We don't count the pickup, so there are 16 measures. This is one of the shortest Chopin pieces in existence, which is good for our task of memorizing. Short pieces are easier due to the limitations imposed on human memory by the nature of our brains. The Chopin Preludes are short; none of them are longer than 90 bars (this one is 17). *Prelude No. 9* is only 12 bars, so our piece is the second shortest.
5. Lyrics. None. So, we have to rely on tone and rhythm memory hooks to help us know if we are playing correctly. I will learn to hum the melody as a memory hook. Try this. Humming or singing the melody is very effective as a memory tool. In popular pieces where there are lyrics, I memorize the lyrics and think of them as I play. This technique is extremely effective for cementing the memory and securing the performance.
6. Fermi estimation. You have to decide this for yourself based on your experience. As for me, I think it will

take at least 2 hours and not more than 5 hours. That gives a product of 10, and the square root is 3.16 hours.
7. Patten estimation. 28 x 6.75 = 189 minutes or about 3 hours.
8. History. Wow! Lots of information about this. Chopin was in debt to his banker Ley, who was demanding payment. Chopin was also ill from the tuberculosis that would eventually kill him, and he was having trouble with George Sand, his lover. It was raining a lot, the roof was leaking, and the weather was unseasonably cold. Furthermore, his favorite piano hadn't arrived at Valldemossa. We know all this from his letters. Since the commission from Camille Pleyel was to create a prelude in each major and minor key, following the circle of fifths, the shorter the better—short pieces would satisfy the contract and get him the payment of 2,000 Francs sooner.

So, why is this Opus 28, No. 7? Opus 28 refers to the preludes. The first is in C major, the second in A minor (the relative minor of C major), the third in G major, and then the famous *E Minor Prelude* as No. 4. Next is D major, followed by B minor as No. 6, and finally A major as No. 7. Those who have played the preludes know that most of them are sad. *E Minor* and *B Minor* were even played on the organ at Chopin's funeral. This one, however, is one of the happy preludes. I imagine the day Chopin worked on this piece, the rain stopped, the sun came out, and maybe Sand kissed him. You should experiment with how you play it. Sometimes, late at night, I play it slow and serious, like a nocturne. Experiment with this piece using different styles. I've even heard it played as a mazurka, which it isn't.

PIANO BY HEART COMPANION

Analysis and Plan of Attack

Recall the limitation of human short-term memory to seven items forward. Therefore, you must work in small sections. Make up your mind you are going to pick and work on short sections. There is no other way. Of course, there is no harm in warming up before you start to work on memorizing. My usual warm up is to play the piece from notes twice. What's yours?

Place memory and image memory are very strong in humans so I will use the position on the sheet as a memory tool and take one line at a time measure by measure. Once a pattern is discovered I will use the pattern as a memory tool. I also like narrative as a memory tool so I will try to use that by making up stories about how the piece is put together. The narrative need not be right or wrong as long as it helps the memory. Remember the brain likes exact repetition and doesn't like variations. Keep the fingering the same throughout the piece. Do not play the same phrase differently each time. Keep hand positions and body postures the same. Otherwise, the brain may get confused and then mess you up. Seal your zeal and get ready for a challenge. Avoid rote. Simply playing the piece over and over again won't work well. Rote repetitions will not get you where you wish to be. Rote is not attentive. You have to be attentive and you must think. Memorization happens, not in your hands, but in your brain. Hours spend playing and replaying without being mentally engaged, will not work. Stop all effort when your brain is tired and do something else until it is refreshed and ready to work. The brain can only take so much.

Conscious and unconscious associations of touch, sound, and sight will help. The more solid these associations are the more likely it is that your performance will not break down. Make sure you understand the larger structure of the piece. I see this prelude as two parts. Do you?

BERNARD M. PATTEN

When you know the larger structure, a few wrong notes or wrong rhythm won't matter because there will be very little adverse effect on the over-all performance. Most audiences are kind and will forgive mistakes and most won't notice a few mistakes if you keep smiling and keep playing on. That is part of showmanship and stage presence.

Don't worry about a practice that goes poorly. Often after a good night's sleep, the memory which was shaky will be firm. Sleep firms up the memories. During sleep the brain cleans itself and works on encoding significant things that you did during the day. As a neurologist, I know this for a fact.

YouTube: I love YouTube and my love is sincere. I like to review what the YouTubers do to the piece I am working on. What is their approach and how can I use it in my work. Some YouTubers are quite funny. One has been working on my current piece (*Chopin Waltz 64 no.2*) for five years and still considers it a work in progress. His discussion of the items he has had trouble with reminded me that I am not alone. Those parts are exactly the parts that are troubling me.

Video: When I finished perfecting this Chopin piece in A major, I made a video of it. The video helped correct my poor posture and some elements of expression. Once I was satisfied, I put a video on my YouTube channel Bernard Patten. You might consider doing the same after you have perfected this Chopin prelude. YouTube gives me a report each month on the number of views, how long the piece has been watched and where it was watched. Most of my viewers are in the United States, England, and India. The viewers often offer helpful comments to aid you in improving. One viewer from Germany said I use too much pedal. On viewing my own videos, I find he is exactly right. Pedal will be something I will improve thanks to that viewer.

PIANO BY HEART COMPANION

Ready? Let's begin memorizing Chopin, *Prelude in A Major*.

Line 1: starting note is E. I will remember that by imagining a memory hook. The piece is A major so it would not be unusual for the first note to be the V note which would be an E.

Let M=measure. M1 – bass is E and top note C#. The C# leads into D so I will make a narrative hook by saying C# is the lead tone to get to D. C# has a time value three times that of the D. The pattern of three-to-one on beat one is found in measures 1, 3, 5, 7, 9, 11, 13, 15. Next in this M1 is chord E7. You could play these notes as octaves E-E in the bass or you could adjust the fingering to suit yourself. I prefer playing an E major chord (EG#B) with the right hand and ED with the left. That fingering seems less awkward. That combination is played twice in this measure and played once for two beats in the M2.

M2 is interesting. There is our fundamental chord E7 the same as in M1 with the addition of DF#. How can I memorize the DF#? I take a mental picture of the measure and note the unique position of DF#. And I tell myself this could be the first half of a D major chord. If that is the case, I would expect some kind of A next and that is in fact what we get in M3.

M3 starts with an A in bass and B# (actually I read as C) D# in treble. Chunking the A in bass with B#D# in treble equals A diminished. Did you recognize it? It is followed by the last third of A major (C#E) noting the time ratio three-to-one. That leads into a combination of bass (AE), which I imagine as a minor chord with the middle tone C omitted and (C#A) in treble making a nice A major chord in total played twice but also carried on to M4 the first measure of line 2. Conclusion: So far everything is easy to recall. But to make sure I really know it, I line up five dimes. I play the first line from memory and then from notes. If I am correct, I move a dime away from the pile. I repeat this process – play the line from memory and checking my playing by reading the notes. When I have played the first line from memory five consecutive times, and all dimes are away from the pile I assume I have line 1 memorized and am ready to go on to line two. Repetition cements memory. Do not be afraid to repeat. While repeating, I am paying attention to the sounds and the rhythm and the position of my hands on the key board. All those associations with help with recall. Having fun while cementing the memory will also help. Your emotional attitude to the piece is important and your attitude to memorization is important. If, at this point you don't like what you are doing then STOP. This piece is not for you.

M4 ends with two notes played by the right hand. These are C# and E – the end third of A major. Now we are really cooking because I think the next thing will be some kind of E – probably an E7 like M1. M5 must start with that three-to-one item. In this case, the item starts with E in bass and C#A# in treble. Decoding that combination of notes gives A# diminished followed by a semitone step to the right where C# goes to D and A# goes to B. And then the predicted E7 occurs. This time it is EB in bass and DD in treble. The F# is included to give a partial hint of D major. Mixing notes from D and E and A seems part of the Chopin art in this piece and probably elevates the piece out of the ordinary and into the ethereal realm of redemptive art. This will be the hardest measure for me and you to get because of the F# and the emphasis on F#D in the right hand. Notice how I construct a narrative plot to help me memorize what's what. Labeling something as hard may actually help me remember the item. Next, I expect some kind of A major to follow E. And that is what we get in M7. First play DG# and then go on to M7, which should have the three-to-one trick on beat one.

PIANO BY HEART COMPANION

M7 repeats DG# from M6 with a nice A in bass. The second part of beat one is what I expect: C#A, followed by a nice big A major made of EAE in bass and C#C# octave in treble. Play this until it sounds and feels natural. M8 starts with the same chord. This you may have predicted if you mastered the general pattern of this piece. And you probably should be predicting that the next measure, M9 should be some kind of E7!

In my view, we are now at the end of part I and will go on to part II.

Pretty much the same pattern as the beginning with the E in M8 followed by a slightly E7 in treble. Instead of C#D we get C#D plus a held E in treble and G#. Play this combo a few times recognizing the similarity and difference between this measure and M1. Carry the E7 into M10 and recognize the similarity and difference of M11 to M3. M11 is expansive with AEA in bass and headed upward to the climax in M12. Play M12 several times to get the feel. I usually just expand the left hand to F#C#EF# encoding it in my memory as a kind of F#7. The right hand now plays a wonderful big chord holding A#C# with my thumb and emphasizing the top A#C#. For me the best fingering is thumb for A#C# and third finger on A# at octave and fifth finger of right hand on C#. My index finger fits neatly on the E at the middle of the chord. And what kind of chord are we dealing with? A#C#E is A diminished our old friend. Another way of looking at it is A#C# on top and bottom in treble with the E inserted between. The dynamic sign indicated this climax should be loud. Play this many times to get the feel and look of your hands on the keyboard and get the sounds in your memory. This is the climax of the piece so I usually linger longer on it then it is written.

For me, the rest of the piece is easy to memorize. Note the beat 3 in M12 is A#C# not AC#. This is followed by the same A#C# and B in bass. Again we have the three-to-one trick in M13 and then a nice step wise descent. The descent looks like B minor going to a kind of E7. This descent is very clever. How to explain it? I don't know but B is the V note of E major so some people would claim this is an example of secondary dominance. I just move my thumb from B to A and add a G# to the bass F#D.

The rest is so logical and expected it doesn't require explanation. We expect a form of A major and that is what we get. Using our compare and contrast ideas, we see the rest resembles M6 to M7 but with some differences. The one item of the three-to-one is now C#A followed by grace note A (which is held) followed by A major in extenso. Play this through until you get the memory perfectly and then review and practice the whole piece. It had to end in A major, and it did. Once I got the piece firmly in the memory it stayed there more or less. Errors were completely corrected with just one review and one play from notes.

My actually time to memorize this piece was 162 minutes. It took about the same time to write and rewrite the talk about it. How did you do? My advantage was that I could make a hazy mental picture of each line and I also knew what to expect more or less by my analysis and knowledge of the V and I connections. My mental picture of M12 is not hazy and helps get the dramatic effect I want when I sound it. My peg for the climax chord is the visual image of the fingers on the appropriate notes. Treble is easy to recall if I remember the paired A#C#s with the E in between. In bass, I easily keep my index finger on the E, move my left thumb to F#, my pinky to the F# below and my third finger to C#. This combination feels fine with no strain. To get comfortable you may have to position your right hand closer to the piano than usual and don't forget the third finger of the right hand goes comfortably on A# with finger four hanging in the air.

PIANO BY HEART COMPANION

Did you get the three-to-one trick? Did it help? I get lots of joy playing this piece. How about you? After you play it awhile your play will become automatic without much thinking involved. That is the desired effect of detailed memory work and that is the effect that permits us to exercise our artistic talents and bring the piece alive according to our individual tastes, style, and view.

Final Stage

Play this piece before any audience you can muster. The more you do it, the better it will get and the more you will be relaxed. Get used to the idea that in some performances you will be nervous. As we discussed, your brain when you are nervous, will be in a different state than it was during your practices at home. Even if you played this piece ten thousand times correctly, it is still possible that you will mess up. Be prepared! Follow my advice and look normal. Smile and nod approval. Most people in the audience will not notice any slip up and those who do won't really care. If possible, play through as if nothing happened. Follow my rule: Never go back. Never restart. Instead jump ahead to a place you previously labelled as your life saver. If you do restart, then people will sense something is wrong. Furthermore, it is highly likely you will slip up at the same place you slipped up at before. Here is the key: Even in practice never stop and restart. That gets you in the wrong habit. Learn how to deal efficiently with the slips in practice and you will deal with them better in performance.

Good luck and happy playing!

Ready for more? Let's work on *Für Elise*.

Für Elise is selected as an example of how to study and memorize a piece of music. It is a classic often heard in recitals and at festivals, and it is fun to play. It is almost never heard at professional performances because it is considered too easy. Beethoven called it a Bagatelle, which in French means "trifle." Perhaps that is what Beethoven thought about it. Perhaps not. Think about this: How would you have liked to have composed this "trifle?"

Clearly, to the people who listen to it and to those who play it or memorize it, and probably for the woman to whom it is dedicated, it is not a trifle but an interesting collection of beautiful sound patterns that will be around practice and recital circles for years to come. I include it in my cocktail hour repertoire, and people like it mixed in with popular music. Last time I was in Russia at the Metropole Hotel, a woman played it on the harp, over and over again, during breakfast every day, and nobody seemed to mind. In fact, most people, my wife and I included, thought it went well with the astounding Russian breakfast.

My Bet

Für Elise will not merely outlive the paper it is written on; it will outlive the oils of Picasso, the Sistine Chapel frescoes of Michelangelo, the Parthenon of Praxiteles. My bet is that humans will take *Für Elise* with them in their heads and in their hearts when they leave Earth to pollute some other planet. *Für Elise* is good music. Good music is not only depthless; it is immortal. *Für Elise* is not merely a masterpiece; it is a masterpiece of masterpieces, a timeless masterpiece.

PIANO BY HEART COMPANION

What You Will Get from Memorizing *Für Elise*

Working through this masterpiece of music as an example should give you basic ideas on how to go about actually memorizing not only this but also other pieces of music that you may wish to perform from memory. When we have finished working on *Für Elise*, the discussion will shift to a completely different type of music, a minuet by Mozart.

Student Patten: Mozart played with his art and, as a consequence, his music is more difficult to memorize.

Teacher White: Then again, we may just leave Mozart to you and not review how to memorize his work. The Beethoven example might be enough to set you thinking, and thinking is, after all, the main goal.

Don't Forget the Basics

Without a basic knowledge of music theory (especially the cycle of fifths), scales, and chords, it is unlikely that you will get the full benefit from the following analysis and advice. You need chunking tools to maximize your memory power and to minimize the time and energy spent in memorization. Understanding music theory will also help you play from printed notes (also known as sight reading) as you will be able the chunk the playing tasks more easily by understanding larger and larger items of musical thought and organization.

Some key things to keep in mind will help clue the memory:

1. Lead tone. The lead tone will usually inform you of what comes next. It helps you expect the next item. If

there is a G#, you probably should expect A minor is next or close by because G# leads to A.
2. Five One Four (V I IV): Never forget the V I relation because that relation will serve your memory well. For instance, if you are moving from A minor to something, expect that something will be E major (the V) of F major or some kind of F, maybe its relative minor D minor. Put your hands on A minor. Go a fifth down and what do you get? Answer: F. If you just played E7, expect the next item will probably be A minor.
3. Harmony: There will be a relation between the melody note in the right hand and what is played in the left. Usually, the left hand will be playing at least one note that is identical with what the right hand is playing and that note will be part of a proper major, minor, or diminished chord. This is a great peg clue to help you recall what goes with what. Every little memory trick helps ease the burden of memory and increases the fun of playing.

You could memorize and recite Lincoln's Gettysburg Address without knowing the meanings of the words "add or detract" and without understanding what is in reference by the phrase "last full measure of devotion." And yes, you could probably, after much work and many tears, memorize and recite correctly the whole address in Chinese without knowing the meaning of a single word in the Chinese language. But such a task would be gigantically difficult, as difficult as learning *Für Elise* without knowing the A minor scale (ABCDEFGA) or the relation of E Major to A minor (E Major is the dominant) or understanding the rondo form of ABACA (the large structure of *Für Elise*).

Therefore, the first and probably most important advice that we can give you, and probably the most important specific advice that you can receive from us, is to learn as much as you can about the actual content and structure of music before you attempt to memorize much. At least continue to learn chords and scales as you work along the music memory trail.

A Music Student Prepares

We discussed how training in memory powers must, at the outset, involve the cultivation of confidence in your own powers. If you have managed to get this far in this book, be assured that you are fully capable of doing anything within reason and, indeed, many things that seem to be outside reason. Music memory is not an accidental thing. It is an art and a science and, when properly worked, will result in success. As you memorize this piece and many others, you will develop a full faith and confidence in your music memory and that confidence will go a long way toward preventing memory failures during performances. With lots of performances under your belt, you will find that performing becomes easier and easier. And as you learn to focus your whole heart and soul on the music to the exclusion of all else, you will find the quality of your performance improved, often improved a great deal, much more than you ever expected.

ABOUT FÜR ELISE

◆ ◆ ◆

In preparation for your memory project, find out some interesting facts about Beethoven and *Für Elise* and the legends that surround them both. This will not only improve your memory of the piece by giving you some associations to use as peg items, but it will also make you look like a better, more culturally aware person, and even better, you will be a better, more culturally aware person.

In general, you will always do well to be able to discourse intelligently for three minutes about any piece that you have memorized. Remember that the information that you dig out yourself will be remembered better by you than the information that you get spoon-fed from the work of others, from your teachers, or, for that matter, from this book.

So do the research yourself. Make notes. Think! Your study might include the point of view of the epoch, the time, the country, the conditions of life, background literature, psychology, social position of the composer, customs, manners, ways of living and performing – anything and preferably everything that interests you. All this work on your material will help you to permeate it with your own knowledge and feelings. It will help you produce great art right there in your home or studio or in the concert hall.

Where to Look

Read the internet stuff on the subject, check out the encyclopedias, and consult a textbook of music, of which there are many.

Don't expect us to fill in the historical details for you. That's your job. For instance, don't expect us to tell you that *Für Elise* is probably one of the most popular piano student pieces ever. Don't expect us to tell you that when Ludwig Nohl found the manuscript of *Für Elise* in 1865 (55 years after it was written and 38 years after Beethoven's death) or that Nohl transcribed the illegible handwriting of Beethoven as *Für Elise*, whereas scholars think Nohl just misread the title because Beethoven's handwriting was so terrible. Don't expect us to tell you that we can't verify or refute Nohl's title or the scholarly surmise that Nohl was wrong because the autograph by Beethoven is missing. Why should we get involved in this kind of controversy that leads nowhere? Our job is to help you with memory not to feed you information or misinformation about music history.

Certainly, we are not going to get involved on why Beethoven had such bad luck with women. Nor will we discuss Therese Malfatti to whom Für Elise is probably dedicated. Beethoven was in love with Therese (legend says), and she had accepted his proposal of marriage. But her parents forbade the union. Therese was just one of a long line of women who either refused to marry Beethoven or who, for one reason or another, did not marry him. That Therese is the "Immortal Beloved" addressed in Beethoven's famous letter discovered after his death in 1827 has not been proven - yet.

And don't expect us to get involved in telling you the many ways to play Für Elise. There are strict constructionists who know, or think they know, that the piece must be played exactly as written without alteration, variation, or elaboration. They think the piece particularly beautiful when it is exactly measured; all of the movements stemming from some kind of clockwork, with the playing unpleasantly perfect, being as lifeless as a music box, a player piano, or a computer.

There are the not-so-strict constructionists (mea culpa) who think Beethoven himself never played this piece (or any other piece) the same way twice for that is what a player piano or a computer can and will do, but what a human cannot do, should not do, and will not be fully able to do. We humans tend to give the music the human touch by changing the tempos, making crescendos, and so forth, showing our human face, neutralizing in the process, if we can, and when we can, the high-tech environment that can be so antithetical to full artistic expression and full realization of the redemptive quality of art, especially as displayed in great musical treasures such as Für Elise.

Doctor Patten: I consider the culture of conformity and orthodoxy basically inherent in the 17th century's apprentice process in music education. It can be viewed as a psychologic defense mechanism against uncertainty, a reason not to be creative, a convenient explanation of why you are not creative and why you don't have to think too much – just follow the score.

The Other Kind

And then, there are those really cool people who build, alter, rearrange and compose pieces based on Für Elise, people who create something new and different by expanding and changing what Beethoven did. Take a look at *The Furry Lisa* by Schneider if this idea interests you. Or dial in Sue Keller's rendition of *The Furry Lisa* on YouTube.

And last, don't expect us to tell you facts about this piece. That is your job, to find the facts.

However, by the time you have finished your research work on this subject, you should know the following:

1. That *Für Elise* is merely the popular name for Bagatelle in A Minor, WoO 59 and
2. That WoO is an abbreviation for the German that means without opus number and
3. That Beethoven composed the piece in 1810, reviewed and polished it several times thereafter, and died without having submitted it for publication and

4. That Beethoven's name for the piece is not *Für Elise*, but is Klavierstücke a-moll WoO 59 which is German and means keyboard piece in A minor and
5. That the piece, though labeled a Bagatelle, is a Rondo in the Rondo form ABACA.

HOW TO DO AN ANALYSIS OF *FÜR ELISE*

◆ ◆ ◆

Für Elise has been out of copyright and in the public domain for a long time. Don't let anyone tell you different. A free copy downloaded from the internet in the six pages should be reviewed with our discussion. For an exercise, study the piece for awhile, until you think you get the big structure.

Student Patten: This took me one hour. It might take you ten minutes. It might not.

Don't write anything on the music sheet, but do see if you can work out a map of the piece and how it is structured. Then play it as best you can for another hour. Then listen to as many versions of *Für Elise* as you can get a hold of. There are nice, neatly played versions on YouTube and special professionally played versions on websites devoted to *Für Elise*. CDs of *Für Elise* are available for purchase on Amazon.com and your local library will have some for listening in the library or for borrow. You can listen to the CD anytime anywhere.

Student Patten: As for me, I do my casual listening to the CD in my car. I do my attentive listening at home. I particularly like the Concert Performance Series, which offers not only a CD professionally played, a detailed score, and a slower CD version for more careful analysis, as well as a MIDI program, which you can use to play along with only the left or the right hand versions. Some students do better learning each hand separately, even though neurologists (myself included) would predict that, in the long run, learning both hands together will work better as that is the playback condition.

Teacher White: I agree unless it is Bach.

Doctor Patten: Hands alone? Hands separately? Which is best? Who knows? Find out what works best for you. Some pieces will be more easily learned hands alone and some with hands together. As always, the technique to use is the one that works best for you under the given circumstances. As for me, I learn Bach better hands together, except when I don't.

Check Out the Versions of Für Elise

After listening to the many versions, compare and contrast the better ones of them by looking at similarities and differences. For instance, note the greater dynamic range in Van Cliburn's performance compared to Valentina Lisitsa, whose performance is available for free on FORELISE.COM.

Valentina has a much smaller dynamic range. And while you are at it, notice tempo differences. Van has greater tempo differences. For instance, Van Cliburn plays the ascending A minor arpeggios faster than Valentina. Should you do the same as Van Cliburn? Or should you copy Valentina? Which way pleases you? Also don't forget each of their performances will be different; not even Beethoven played the same piece exactly the same twice. Each of your performances will be different also. And, of course, not all performances are good.

Student Patten: I am my own favorite pianist. Most pianists prefer their own performances to that of others. How about you?

Next Task

Connect with the music on multiple levels: Emotional, Motor, Aural, Visual and Intellectual for these are the big five categories that help with music memory. Memory for music is not, as many people might think, a special kind of memory. Nope. It is a collaboration of the above-mentioned five categories of memory skills that are present in every normal person.

The more levels that you connect with the better your associations will be and the easier it will be for you to encode the piece in your memory. Going over any music will bring in the multiple modalities that we have discussed. Your emotions are dragged in. Your motor memory stimulated. Your aural and visual memories, ditto. For music is a multimodal abstract art. All of music's modalities will, either consciously or unconsciously, take part in what you are doing and the more associations you can make, the stronger will be your long-term memory of the piece.

These memory modalities are leaders of habit (engrained motor and sensory programs), without which no performance is possible. They are a huge orchestra, and a wayward one, whose members are forever playing pranks and delighting in secret and subtle associations. Your conscious intelligence, like a conductor, must direct and control them, their training, demanding, understanding, and enough, but not too much, discipline.

Motor memory, particularly, is an occasional bad actor, impatient of authority, and easily able to upset even the good habits. Even the conscious control mechanism has a bad side: Mind wandering, which can mislead the whole orchestra.

All these modalities, if perfectly trained on a given piece, will perform perfectly, provided that the consciousness does not surrender to nervousness or mind wandering or to telephone call interruptions from the audience.

THE MARRIAGE OF TWO MINDS: CONSCIOUS AND UNCONSCIOUS

◆ ◆ ◆

Success in any mental endeavor is not necessarily dependent on the amount of effort involved. There are degrees of trying, involving more or less effort. Beware of trying too hard, for that usually gets nowhere. For example, if you try too hard to get to sleep, sleep often will not come. (We can't see you right now, but we know some of you are smiling because you have had that experience.)

Try not to be nervous and you might become all the more so. This is the law of reversed effort. No one seems to know why it is a law or how it operates but it does. The general rule is that too much conscious effort may impair unconscious mechanisms and seriously hamper subconscious habits and actions. Trying too hard to play from memory will usually make us make more mistakes than usual. So, there is a necessity for non-interference in brain programs that have been over-learned and are in the subconscious motor programs.

Thinking Too Much Can Be Too Much Thinking

Doctor Patten: An illustration of what we are talking about is that I can tie a bow tie without effort or thought because I have been doing that task for over fifty years. I can tie a bow tie perfectly without thinking about it. And yet, if I do concentrate my attention on the tie or the procedure if I make the mistake of giving attention where none is needed, I will often become flummoxed or get confused or tie a clumsy knot and have to begin again. When I am typing a book manuscript, if I become too intent on preventing errors, if I actually start thinking about what letters to type, I will make an unusual number of errors.

Prove to Yourself That Too Much Thinking Can Foul Up Unconscious Motor Programs

Stand up. Consciously think about walking across the room, putting one foot in front of the other. Notice that your walking has become somewhat stiff and unnatural and probably slower than usual. Now, sit at the piano and play a piece that you know by heart. Somewhere in the middle of that piece, instead of giving attention to what you are playing, consciously think about your technique or think about how well you are doing or think about how much your audience would appreciate the performance. Prediction: you will play badly at that point. The conscious interference that hurt your playing was not caused by fear or nervousness. Nope. The adverse effect was due to switching your stage one consciousness from the read-out activity of getting the music out of stage three to focus attention on an appraisal of your technique. Stage one is limited, as we know, so it became impossible to think about the music and the technique at the same time. Hence the problem. The solution is to recognize that life is made up of habits (mental and physical) that are subconscious and need to be left alone (for the most part) to do their work. Consciousness is but a small part of the musical mind. Behind consciousness is a vastly older and more comprehensive mind, the subconscious and, god help us, the unconscious mind, which can be trusted, and should be trusted, to play its part. Bottom line: There must be an effective marriage of conscious and subconscious mechanisms for effective performance. Relaxing, not trying too hard, and training yourself to focus on the music and nothing else during the performance will help you overcome the difficulties in this convenient marriage and, most times, will prevent serious disagreement and divorce.

The Marriage of Feelings and Intellect

Talking about convenient marriage reminds me of another kind of marriage of convenience, important in performance, but a little nebulous to put in practice and kind of abstract to talk about. It is one thing to feel music and it is another thing to understand it. And yet another thing to speak its language with authority. There are players who exert too little conscious control on their performance, relying almost entirely on emotion. There are cerebral players (too many of them on the current festival circuit) who think so much consciously that they inhibit feeling. The greatest artists exemplify a balance of feeling and intellect. When the two, feeling and intellect, collaborate, the effect is wonderful. This mental poise is something that can be taught and developed and usually comes from great experience in expression, as in the advanced forms of poetry. Try reciting a poem of the Irish poet Yeats. First, recite it as verse and then read it out loud as prose.

Her Anxiety by William Butler Yeats

Earth in beauty dressed
Awaits returning spring
All true love must die
Alter at the best into some lesser thing
Prove that I lie.
Such bodies lovers have
Such exacting breath
That they touch and sigh
With every touch they give
Love is nearer death
Prove that I lie.

Hear the difference? Your prose recital is flat, because these immortal words were written as poetry and need to be recited as verse and not recited as prose.

The same applies to music. Play your piece with your heart and soul in the music and then play like a weary worn-out street piano, mechanical and tired.

Hear the difference? When you don't play with heart and soul, the result can be emotionally flat.

HOW TO EMPLOY MULTIMODALITIES

◆ ◆ ◆

Very well then, we have discovered that you can't isolate the various modalities of music memory as they tend to run together and work together. But we can call our attention to each one, one at a time by focusing. They are the big five and they are the items that will help you the most get *Für Elise* into your memory. Let's start with the emotional level.

Emotional Level

Does *Für Elise* suggest any emotions to you? When studying a piece of music it is probably not possible to inhibit the feelings that the music seems to provoke. If music had any emotion at all – and it would be a pretty poor piece of music that does not contain some suggestion of emotion – you will find that emotion stealing upon you despite your best efforts to disregard it. You might just as successfully try reading Macbeth without feeling the error of overvaulting ambition or without feeling the sweep of the verse as Macduff cries, "Despair thy charm! MacDuff was from his mother's womb untimely ripped."

Teacher White: I believe music has no emotion, but the performance of music will decide if and what emotion is present. We create the story and the emotion when we play.

Doctor Patten: Come to think on it, Jimmy is probably right. There probably is no emotion in music, as there is no emotion in sound per se. The emotion is put there by the people making the music and by the people listening to the music. The emotion is a work-product of the human brain. In the same way, there is no color in this wide world. Yes, there is no color. That is a scientific fact: The world is gray. The color that we think we see is purely a product of the human brain, which takes three primary wavelengths of light (which we call red, blue, and green) and combines them in proportions to give us the illusion of color, the illusion of 23 million colors. In fact, many animals do not see color, and some humans are color blind as well. All humans are color blind in subdued light because the cones do not function under conditions of low light intensity. Protanopes have a gene that gives their long-wavelength cones the medium-wavelength pigment by mistake. Those people see green when they should see red, and they see green when they should see green. Deuteranopes have a gene that gives their medium-wavelength cones the long-wavelength pigment by mistake. Those people see red when they should see green and they see red when they should see red. Thus, both the protanopes and deuteranopes have trouble telling green from red and will have difficulty getting a license to drive. Amazingly, some people have both genes. These reverse trichromats can therefore see green and red, but reversed. The qualia normal people know as red would be green to them and vice versa.

Use the Emotions That You Get from *Für Elise* to Remind Yourself of the Piece

Are there parts of *Für Elise* that suggest hesitation? Gloom and doom? Hops and jumps? Death? Persistent exhortation? Joy? Play? Tension and release? Anger? Contemplation? The reek of cold wet stone? Yearning? Gentle, soft youth? Thunder and lightning?

A case could be made for such things. Whether these and other emotions are actually in the music or not in the music is debatable (See the notes above). Emotion exists without reason and is not generally regarded as a logical thing. Some people feel it; others don't. Emotion and reason exist on different parallel planes that may never meet. Nevertheless, emotion has a logic of its own and neuroscience tells us that the right hemisphere of our brains is more emotional and in control of emotional expression than is the left hemisphere, which is more specialized for logic and language.

The key point is that if the music of Für Elise seems to suggest emotional things to you, then the emotions suggested can be used as a framework, as a matter of study, as a chunking or association tool, as a name or label or what have you, clues, cues, and pegs to help you organize your memory of the piece.

Use Emotional Associations to Construct a Narration of How the Piece Progresses

Student Patten: What follows is just an example of how I might use my emotional associations to construct a working narration model of the musical treasure we now know as Für Elise. The narration you do for yourself will serve you better than any narration made for you by someone else. So, review Doctor Patten's narration for some ideas on how to construct your narration of *Für Elise,* and then do a narration on your own.

Doctor Patten's Narration of *Für Elise*

For instance, to me part A seems to have two main themes that alternate with each other. Hence, I will call Theme One "Theme A1" and I will call Theme Two "Theme A2."

Doctor Patten's Narration of *Für Elise*

To me, part A of *Für Elise* seems to have two main alternating themes, so I'll refer to the first as Theme A1 and the second as Theme A2.

Theme A1: This opening theme starts with an arpeggiated figure that's simple yet expressive. To my ear, it sounds as if someone is hesitating, as though pondering a question that hasn't yet been answered. The mood is tentative and uncertain and evokes an image of someone at the beginning of an emotional journey. This part of the piece has always felt like a quiet monologue, perhaps a private conversation with oneself. The rising and falling arpeggios suggest a deep, but personal contemplation. Imagine someone walking alone in a garden, stopping to admire a flower and then moving on, unsure of what they're looking for.

In memory terms, I associate Theme A1 with "questioning" or "yearning."

Theme A2: The second theme is bolder and more playful. Here, we encounter a melodic pattern that feels almost like an answer to the hesitation of Theme A1. It's as if someone has found their answer or at least has decided to throw caution to the wind. The sound becomes more confident, with an added bounce and lightness, like someone dancing lightly after making a decision. To me, this theme could be thought of as a "resolution" or "reassurance" after the uncertainty of the first theme. It feels uplifting, suggesting that perhaps the protagonist of this musical story has found some clarity.

I associate Theme A2 with "playfulness" or "resolve."

Transitioning Between the Themes

When these two themes are juxtaposed, you can imagine the constant shift in the emotions of the character: questioning followed by moments of confidence, only to retreat back into reflection. This ebb and flow of emotional tension provides a natural dynamic to the piece, and it's important to feel this when playing the music. Think of it as a conversation with oneself where thoughts and emotions alternate between doubt and confidence.

The "B" Section (Part B):

Then comes Part B, which diverges significantly from the A section. This middle section feels like a contrast to the earlier alternating thoughts of A1 and A2. Part B has a stronger, more determined feeling. I envision it as a change in emotional tone—the hesitation and introspection from Part A are temporarily replaced by a more assertive attitude.

The passage in B starts to rise with force and motion, hinting at a sense of urgency or even frustration. The rolling bassline and broader, more assertive melody convey a sense of striving or confrontation with an obstacle. It's almost as if the character is faced with a challenge or a sudden burst of energy. The piece takes on a bolder stance here—this isn't the quiet contemplation of Theme A1, but rather a more driven push forward.

For Part B, my emotional association is "striving" or "determination."

Return to the A Theme (Part A – Reprise)

After Part B, we return to the familiar A theme, but it feels different upon reintroduction. After the brief confrontation or burst of energy in Part B, coming back to A1 feels like a return to the self. The mood is softer, as if the character is tired from their exertion in B. This repetition of the original theme feels like a reflection on the journey that's just taken place. Now, the piece is tinged with more experience, possibly more wisdom.

The A1 theme now can be associated with "reflection" after the emotional and energetic journey of Part B.

Emotional Structure of *Für Elise*

To summarize, the emotional structure I use for memory is:

1. Theme A1 (Tentative, Questioning, Yearning)
2. Theme A2 (Playfulness, Resolve, Reassurance)
3. Part B (Striving, Determination, Challenge)
4. Theme A1 (Reflection, Experience, Softened Reprise)

By anchoring each section of *Für Elise* to an emotion or an image, you can create a narrative that makes the music easier to remember. The emotions act as mnemonic devices to help connect the notes with something familiar and relatable, enhancing both your memory and your performance.

Conclusion

This narrative approach to *Für Elise* has helped me build a deeper connection to the music and improved my ability to play it from memory. Creating your own emotional associations, whatever they may be, can do the same for you. Just as with any piece, your interpretation will be unique, and that's where the beauty lies.

Now, take these ideas, construct your own narrative, and see how much they enhance your memorization of *Für Elise*.

Theme A1 starts with the chromatic hesitation between E and D# (circled in red; measures 1 & 2), which goes to A in measure 3 via a nice descent E-B-D-C (blue box; measure 2). E goes to B because B is the V note of E. E-B-D-C is a poem that rhymes. Play it a few times until it rings in your head. The A note in measure 3 should remind me that the bass also plays an A note to start an A minor chord, which I call a fifth chord because it consists of two fifths – A to E and E to A. This is A minor without the middle tone.

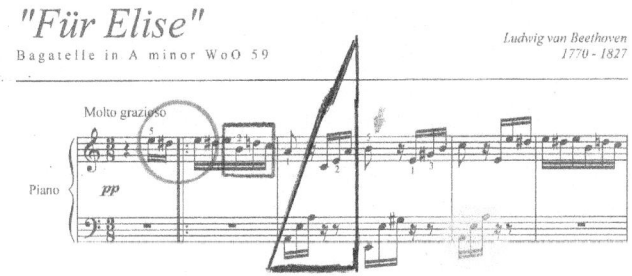

That triggers an A minor arpeggio ascent (outlined by the large black triangle; measure 3), which leads to the upper B (green arrow; measure 4), triggering an E Major arpeggio ascent in measure 4 (not outlined), which leads back to A minor (colored yellow; measure 5). Then hit the E in the second half of measure 5 and start the E-D# sequence and the arpeggios again.

PIANO BY HEART COMPANION

Play these on the piano. Block out the chord notes with both hands to get a feel for the hand positions and note how it sounds. Pretty good, right? Playing theme A1 is fun and relatively easy—easy to play and easy to memorize, especially if you've listened to it many times on the CDs and can hum the music in your head.

Theme A2 starts with a nice sequence of four ascending notes (B-C-D-E) (green box; measure 10 and part of measure 11) and then continues with a sequence where G jumps to F-E-D, followed by the same sequence a step down (F jumps to E-D-C), then again a step down (E jumps to D-C-B), followed by a neat set of bounces from low E to high E. Try playing these and see what I mean. Don't bother worrying too much about individual notes. Just remember to start at B and go up one note at a time, playing four notes (including B). Then recall the jump down to G, and from G, jump up just shy of an octave to F and descend by two notes. Now repeat the same pattern, starting on E and jumping to D-C-B. Hit B with the lowest E, and you're ready to start jumping up again. Notice the two E's in the middle that repeat.

Reminder: The narration you create for yourself will serve you better than the narration I provide. Sit and think! Work on your way of organizing the music.

BERNARD M. PATTEN

But what about the left hand? What's it doing?

The left hand is following the right by finding the right chords for good harmony. So, during the ascending sequence B-C-D-E, the left hand plays E with a C, and then it continues to play G. (This is the C chord (E-C-G) in its second inversion.) The same pattern continues: the note you end on in the right-hand descent is always part of the chord being played as an arpeggio in the left hand. Work this out for yourself to be sure of the patterns and to understand the ideas that help you get the sequence correct. The left hand sequence consists of C arpeggios, then G arpeggios, and then A minor arpeggios. First C, then G, and then A minor is the way I remember it, along with a firm picture of my hand on the chords in the correct sequence.

Study the illustrations below if you don't quite understand what happens with the jumping E's. If you do understand, skip the illustrations and focus on the feeling of the keys and the sequence.

The sequences and the fact that the bounces involve only E's make this an easy part to play and remember. Note that the high B at the green arrow is played with E in the left hand. This is easy to remember because B is the fifth note of the E major chord, and the two notes, B and E, sound good together. That sets off the sequence of jumping E's that move from the low end of the piano to the high end. The jumping E's are outlined in a red parallelogram. Note that middle E is played three times, but the best way to handle this is to play the arpeggio going up on E-E-E, then play middle E and the E an octave higher twice, and finally play the high E and another E an octave still higher. Right after that, you're back in familiar territory with theme A1, starting with our old friend E-D#.

Tickle the Ivories to Get a Feel for the Music

Of course, it's much easier to look at the keys and get the feel for what should be played and when rather than memorizing each and every note in the two themes. Kids usually have no trouble getting the hang of the opening two themes. Playing these themes is not only easy but also fun and will impress most audiences, especially at cocktail parties. But don't be a slouch. Don't just play the easy part—learn the entire piece by tackling the hard and stormy sections of *Für Elise*.

APPROACHING THE HARD PARTS WITH EQUANIMITY

◆ ◆ ◆

Into every life, a little rain must fall, and now, like it or not, it's raining cats and dogs on you—because right after the easy Themes A1 and A2, which make up part A of *Für Elise*, comes part B: the hard part.

To me, part B has a song-like quality, so I consider the first section of B a song, while the second section seems like an opportunity to show off, especially at high speed. I call that the "show-off" section. Thus, applying the

Roman rule of divide and conquer, I will dissect section B into two parts: B Hard (the difficult part of B) and B Easy (the easier, show-off section of B). But you may call these B1 and B2 if you like.

B1 starts with a cadence that is easy:

The cadence is introduced by the DCB trichord (blue circle; measure 23) The trichord DCB (blue circle; measure 23) is followed by the right-hand A and left-hand A minor arpeggio (yellow patch; measure 25), which should now be familiar. The actual cadence (outlined in the black box; measure 25) starts with what looks like a C7 (the B-flat CEC is the tip-off), then goes to F and back to C7. The last C7 is the same as the first but with the addition of G in the treble and G in the bass. Naturally, when entering the cadence, we don't play measure 24 again, which is why it has been crossed out with a big red X.

Play the cadence as often as you need to in order to get it into memory. Note the initial position of your hands at the start and memorize how it feels and looks to play that first rousing C7. Once you can play the cadence from memory without difficulty, take a short break and walk around the room. Reward yourself in some way because the brain takes rewards quite seriously and will perform better when rewarded. When you feel relaxed and rested, come back for a further discussion of *Für Elise*.

By the way, some versions have the cadence staccato. Play it as you choose!

Welcome back!

B Hard is complex, with seven difficult measures, so we will have to spend time and go through many repetitions to get it into our memories. We will talk more about it later.

B Easy is easier and will be especially easy if we recognize the patterns involved. Meanwhile, keep in mind that although section B has given thousands of students millions of headaches, those students—some of them, anyway—have eventually gotten over the headaches and mastered the section. If generations of students before you could memorize and play section B reasonably well from memory, so can you.

After showing off by playing B Easy, we need a rest, so we repeat Theme A1 twice, Theme A2 once, and then Theme A1 twice again.

That's easy to recall: Theme A1 is played twice, Theme A2 is played once, and then Theme A1 is played twice again. If it's Theme A1, it's played twice. If it's Theme A2, it's played once. Get it?

This pattern is similar to and different from what happened at the beginning, where Theme A1 went on four times (more or less, with minor variations), and Theme A2 went on twice.

Thus far, the structure of *Für Elise* runs like this:

Theme A1 repeated four times, more or less
Theme A2 repeated twice
Section B (hard song part followed by show-off easy part)
Theme A1 twice
Theme A2 once
Theme A1 twice

All the repeats are nice and easy but somewhat boring, so Beethoven gets "depressed" and starts hammering on that low A as if it were a tom-tom.

Whether the last sentence is true or not is debatable. But what is true is that by imposing the idea of the tom-tom and relief from boring repetition onto the piece, it helps recall what Section C is about, and that recall will help you remember when and where to play Section C. I have witnessed recitals where C is completely eliminated (mea culpa), and no one except the teachers seemed to notice.

The idea behind the purpose of Section C may also color how that section is played. Your interpretation of Section C will shape your performance, so be careful how you select your memory hooks and memory pegs. Misinterpretations could result in a stylish faux pas, coloring your performance the wrong way.

Section C itself has two parts, which I call C1 and C2. C1 can be divided into two parts as well, so we call them C1a and C1b:

C1a: the tom-tom in the bass and fireworks in the treble, which more or less repeats something similar in C1b, which is an imitation of C1a: tom-tom in the bass and fireworks (thunder and lightning) in the upper register. The entire C section is complex, so we will have to spend time and repetition to get it into our memories. We will talk more about it later. Keep in mind, though, that this section has given thousands of students millions of headaches—but they eventually got over it, and some of them mastered it. If they could memorize and play it, so can you.

Then we get another show-off section, which is easy, consisting of A minor arpeggios ascending, followed by that chromatic descent. This is our reward for wading through C1a and the C1b imitation of C1a. Once you know C1 (both sections) and C2, I predict you will enjoy playing it and putting your own touch and personal style into the performance.

Section C is fair game for individual expression.

Having listened to multiple CD performances of Section C, we concluded that this is the section where people play it their own way. Some renditions play C very loudly, while others play it softly. There are several renditions where the dynamics shift: loud in C1, soft in the imitation of C1, and loud again in C2, and vice versa. There are also versions with C played slowly, others played quickly, and several in between. Listen to as many versions as you can and decide what suits you best.

Student Patten: As for me, I like to play it softly and slowly, but sometimes, for reasons known only to God, when the mood strikes, I'll break out and play it loudly and quickly—and like it just as much as when I played it the other way. Perhaps this ability of the same music to somehow fit our mood and satisfy us is one of the qualities that makes it great. What do you think?

HEADED INTO THE HOMESTRETCH

◆ ◆ ◆

Whew! That was fun, and now we're in the homestretch with Theme A1 twice, Theme A2 once, Theme A1 once, and then a coda, which is almost the same as Theme A1, but modified slightly to serve as a coda, fading out on (where else) the tonic A (enclosed in the pink teardrop squiggle; measure 106). (Note: Some versions have C-A in the treble plus the octave A's in the bass. Choose what you prefer.)

Hints and Discussion:

Emotion

The emotional modality is probably the least useful for memorizing music, but the invention of a narrative flow based on some emotions is useful. Try it.

PIANO BY HEART COMPANION

About memorizing by emotion: Do not proceed too rigidly or in a mechanical way. There is no single one way to understand and retain new information. There is no single device to use in every situation where new knowledge or memory would be helpful. And yet, as mentioned, experts in education tell us that one of the most powerful ways to learn new material is from stories. We seem as humans to respond profoundly to narratives, and to extract from certain tales key lessons that become the basis of future learning. The narratives that have the most significance for us are the ones that strike an emotional chord. So instead of a mechanical and tired narrative we need to image one that has an emotional significance for us. For instance, in *Für Elise* do not say that the initial chromatic hesitation (ED#) is resolved by the decisive and triumphant arpeggios in A minor and E major that follow. That's an intellectual analysis with an intellectual narrative. Do not tell yourself that the rumbles in A that introduce section C are mitigated by the chromatic return to part A, resolving the harsh and conflicting moods of section C. That's intellectual also but with some emotional flavors mixed into the narrative.

OK, do tell yourself that stuff if it suits you and you like to talk and think like that. But in our way of thinking, what's more important is to observe how and why the seeming changes in emotion are brought about (pitch is elevated, tempo accelerated, major happy chords are exchanged for minor sad chords or diminished chords, and so forth). Emotional analysis is of service when employed in conjunction with the other aids to memory or when built into a narrative flow. Otherwise, emotion analysis by itself is of little value.

Doctor Patten: My own private opinion is that there is no emotion in music except that our thinking and feeling makes it so. My wife Ethel says A1 and A2 are erotic and suggest passion and romance and even sex to her.

Motor Level

Does the piece provoke motor movements? Where and what kind? In dance form pieces, this may be more obvious. But see if *Für Elise* set your foot tapping or your arms swinging. Finger movement at various passages would be a good sign that motor memory is ready to help you memorize this piece.

Aural

After you have heard the music many times, the music may start to play itself in your head. This is a good thing and should not cause alarm. Most people will hum the tune after they have heard it a few repetitions.

Student Patten: If my wife Ethel, who has little or no musical skill to speak of (just like me), can do this, so can you. The ability to hear the actual music in your head is just a natural extension of the humming phenomenon. With me the phenomenon first occurred after I had listened to Rhapsody in Blue a number of times. I thought I had turned the CD player off and was annoyed that the music had continued. Imagine my surprise when I discovered the CD player was off! The music was playing itself in my head!

Yes, the music was coming from inside my head. Subsequently, I have learned to control the music by making it louder or softer, and of course, I can turn it off. If you can hear a whole orchestra in your head, you would be a fool not to take advantage of that skill in memorizing your pieces. The concert pianist, Ray Alston, hears the music in his head and follows the melody. What works for him might work for you.

Start the music in your head and then play along in your head as you please. Good music and even second-rate music is like that – easily memorized by ear. Its tuneful melody and its sheer original sound attract the ear, and for that reason, the music remains in the mind. Sometimes, it remains in the mind for too long, and people complain that they can't stop it or get rid of it. For some reason, this phenomenon is called an earworm.

Teacher White: Depends on the type of melody and the people involved.

Aural Memory Starts with Melody Most of the Time

In memorizing by ear, start with the melody. Sit there with the notes and sing or hum the piece. Then, without the notes, sing again. As soon as you feel you have gone off, look at the notes. Discover the place you went wrong and try to figure out why. Sing again repeatedly – twenty times or more – concentrating on the troubling passage.

Test yourself on the whole piece from time to time. When you can sing or hum the entire piece from memory, then place the notes before you and visualize them or some of them with your eye as per instructions below under the heading visual. Eye and ear work well together. What one misses the other supplies. Memorizing harmony by ear is a whole different matter and is usually too difficult to do by ear and too time-consuming to do, period. Harmony can be better done by intellect by which we mean conscious association and analysis.

Aural memory is particularly helpful in memorizing some modern pieces, some of which have no emotion to speak of.

Student Patten: Usually, I can't discover any emotion in Schoenberg or Webelen, and yet, after a number of repetitions, I can hum them, and after a lot of repetitions, I can play them in my head. On the other hand, there are certain kinds of music whose melodic line is so broken or is so faintly indicated or is of so bare a nature that, in memorizing it, it is safer to rely on motor memory, intellectual memory, and visual memory. For me, Mozart is that way. I take little pleasure in Mozart because, in spite of its grace and flow, it seems that the soul of the music is often absent. His minuets are easy to remember and easy to forget because, in essence, they are sexless. That is why the emotionally cold people are so appreciative of Mozart. We hear the luscious melody. Who can't? But it doesn't seem to have any groundage: it flies away on the whitest and flimsiest of clouds. It gives a moment of pleasure and is gone. Rarely does it return the spirit of delight. If by chance it does return, it sounds a little grotesque, full of fuzz and bumble with violent panjandrumese of the stage (as in Don Juan) or the poppycock of Figaro. Mozart, playing with his gift, makes it difficult for us to memorize by aural associations alone and forces us to use intellect, motor memory, and visual memory.

Teacher White: Some of this is right, and some of it is rubbish. Patten doesn't see things the way real musicians (like me) do. Mozart is wonderful. Because he does the unexpected, some people are turned off and don't understand Mozart's true genius. Mozart may have had Attention Deficit Hyperactivity Disorder, but so what? He likes to play with his music and have some fun. Das ist gut.

Visual

Would it surprise you to know that there are people who can actually visualize the musical score in their head and then read the notes out from the visualized score? Such people would be fools not to use that skill in helping to memorize music. There is a way to develop this kind of eidetic imagery, but it takes practice and concentrated effort. In our view and for us, the results are not as good as working with aural clues.

Student Patten: My problem is that it takes time to summon the score before my mind's eye and then it takes time to read the notes from that score – too much time for the technique of visualizing the whole score to be an effective tool for me in performance. But I do get help by visualizing individual measures that are complex or that are at critical junctions in the piece. Many of these images of individual measures reappear just as I am about to fall asleep, with every note looking clear, proof that my brain has stored the image and has been subconsciously "thinking" about it. Eidetic images of certain measures are of secondary importance to my main use of visual memory. My main use of visual memory is by actually picturing where my hands and fingers should be on the piano at a given point in the piece. I do this by placing my hands and fingers in the proper position and studying them long enough to fix the mental image of their positions. So *when Für Elise* starts, I have a good image of where my fingers should be to start playing the ED#, just as I have a very clear-cut image of where my hands should be when I start playing the cadenza to introduce part B of the piece.

Always memorize where your hands should be positioned especially at the beginning of a piece and at the beginning of each section of a piece. Position and the image of your hands (and their feel) on the keys are important peg tools to help recall.

Memory of where and how the hands and fingers are positioned for play will augment the intellectual understanding and analysis of the piece and will support aural and motor memories. Make up your mind right now that you are going to sit down at the piano and memorize the exact position of your hands at the beginning of each of the major sections of *Für Elise*. Test yourself on these to make sure that you really know them. Where is the starting position of A? Where are your hands and fingers for the start of B? And so forth. Prove to yourself that you actually know it by actually doing it right.

How to Develop Your Visual Memory Modality

Doctor Patten: It is with hesitation that I give hints to you on how to develop music memory by way of the visual modality. These ideas will then be illustrated by my showing how to use visual memory of the important measures in *Für Elise*. The visual image of those important measures (usually the beginning and end of sections) will be augmented by an aural association with the visualized measure and an analytic or intellectual association of the same measures. Thus, I will summon several memory modalities to help me with the hard measures.

Before we start let me announce that my experience with this training has been with patients and not with music students so what I say here may not even have an application to music. Yet I think it does. Also, be warned that most musicians who claim to have a photographic memory for music do not have that skill. They are recognizing patterns and memorizing the patterns using a visual mnemonic. Don't believe me? Ask a musician who claims a photographic memory to memorize a page of random notes. She can't. Ask that same musician to memorize a 20-page sonata. She can.

PIANO BY HEART COMPANION

THE VISUAL MODALITY

◆ ◆ ◆

Select the piece you wish to memorize by eye. The more unusual the visual image of the music sheet, the better. Look at the measures bar by bar without playing any on the piano. Gaze at the first bar for five minutes. Yes, that is what I said: five minutes. Do not play the melody in your head and do not do any kind of analysis. You are examining the bar with your eyes only. When you think that your visual system has taken on the image of the bar as a whole, close your eyes and try to summon the image before your mind. The brain is making images all the time and will be able to make an image of music if you let it – if you let it. There is a gigantic cultural prejudice against making this type of visual image because it has been associated with schizophrenia and other forms of severe mental illness.

Above all do not be frightened when the image comes and is seen in your mind's eye. You are not going crazy. You are just learning to use a part of your visual memory that is not often used in our culture and is in fact often suppressed in our educational systems. Albert Einstein (perhaps you have heard of him) shows the process in his autobiographical notes and was a master at imagining visual images. He then used these images (lightning flashes, moving trains, golden cages accelerated in space, and so forth) to solve complex problems in relativity theory, problems that other physicists were not able to solve. If Einstein used mental images to advantage, so can you.

BERNARD M. PATTEN

Our Ancient Ancestors Used Visual Images to Advantage to Remember Complex Material

Doctor Patten: In ancient times most of the memories were encoded by making mental images. For those of you who might be interested in this technique, I have listed books on the subject, plus my own scientific papers. The book by Frances Yates, *The Ancient Art of Memory*, is considered the classic in this field. My paper published in *Neurology* (the official journal of the American Academy of Neurology) has a reasonably short history of this ancient art.

Exercises in Making Visual Images

The first few attempts may result in failure. So what. That is normal. Keep working. A half hour a day for a month will produce excellent results. Usually, in the beginning of your work, the sheet music will reappear, actually popup, in your head just as you are about to go to sleep. Do not be frightened by this as it is not a psychotic hallucination but the very effect you have been working to achieve. The official medical term for this image is hypnopompic hallucination. It is normal. Instead of worrying about it, learn to use it to your advantage.

With the music picture in your mind, try to manipulate the image. Enlarge it or make it smaller. Project it onto the adjacent wall and whirl it about. These exercises will increase your power to visualize and revisualize. The exercises will give you ideas on how to use the image in your performance. During your attempts to make the mental music images, you will probably discover means of your own that will help with your visual music memory. If you do develop a good technique be sure to let us know so we can use it ourselves or share it with others in the next edition of this book.

Succorance for the Faint of Heart

To those of you who had a sinking feeling when you read the above advice from Doctor Patten and to those of you that said to yourself that it is of no use to you, or worse, to those of you who said to yourselves or thought "This is nutty, really nutty." The reply is that you must understand that visualization is very common. It is hard to believe that any student is entirely without this gift. If you don't think that it is common, then start your visualization work with common objects around the home. Doctor Patten's favorite for teaching patients visualization was a coke bottle. Usually the patients would be able to eventually see the image of the coke bottle in their minds' eye. After that, some of them could actually see the image in the external visual space as if the coke bottle were a holographic image. Then some could learn to project the coke bottle image onto a white wall and enlarge and contract the image as they see fit and whirl it as well. As mentioned, the first sign of significant progress is the popup appearance of the coke bottle just before the onset of sleep. One patient even called at night to complain that the coke bottle was haunting him by appearing and disappearing just before sleep. If you don't want to start with visualizing a coke bottle, try making a mental image of your home, your room, or the face of a person you love. You will discover that you are not entirely without the power of visualization and you will discover that that power, like any other brain skill, will develop with concentrated effort.

BERNARD M. PATTEN

INTELLECTUAL

◆◆◆

The intellectual modality is the one we like best because it is the one under conscious control. It is possible using conscious control to memorize a piece by intellect alone. To do so would be a great intellectual achievement. But we are not out to make a great intellectual achievement. We are out to make memorization as simple and as easy as possible and fun. The intellectual modality, therefore, is a support to the other modalities that we mentioned (emotion, motor, aural, visual). But, in fact the main support of the memory encoding of the large structure of the piece is the intellectual analysis. ABACA keeps you on track to play *Für Elise*.

The trouble with analysis on an intellectual level is that it can be bone dry and boring, as you will soon see when we go through the analysis of the difficult sections of *Für Elise*. It is also somewhat difficult to meld the intellectual analysis with the other modalities that we discussed, particularly with the emotions. For it seems to us that intellect works best for us. But for you, maybe something else is better. Much depends on the psychology of the particular individual student.

Doctor Patten: A pseudo-scholar like myself must start with the intellectual approach as that is what I do best. What you use as your primary approach to memory is up to you. Choose as you wish. For me, the motor memory backs up my intellectual understanding of the piece and the aural rendition of the piece in my mind supports both the motor memory and the intellectual analysis. For me, there isn't any point to putting *Für Elise* into a mental picture of the score. Why should I when I can play the whole thing in the aural modality in my mind? But I will use visual memory at critical junctures in the piece to support my intellect and aural associations. Those critical junctions will be the transitions between parts A and B and A and C, and for those parts, I will have a firm picture of where my hands should be on the keyboard and what they should be doing there. The last and least useful modality of music memory for me is emotions. Yes, there are probably some emotions expressed in *Für Elise*, but my psychiatry training prevents me from identifying them as real or significant. Instead of (a bunch of fake?) emotions expressed, I hear collections of beautiful sound patterns. So, for me, it is easier to organize my memory of the piece by appreciating the beauty and organization of the abstract sound patterns than to assign an emotional significance to the patterns. I am not saying the emotions are not there or could not be put there by some performer or some listener: I am saying emotions are not that useful for me in memorizing the piece. Others will create an emotion or a story with emotion to guide them through the piece. The narration and the emotions attached to the narration may be useful as peg items, but in that case the emotional items are being placed into the intellectual, that is, the conscious realm.

Thinking About the Piece Is the Starting Point of Intellectual Analysis

Intellectual analysis must be critical even with the work of the greatest composers. Most important is to ask why? Why? Why? Why? In intellectual analysis you don't just swallow what you are given on the sheets, you always ask what is going on here and how did the composer handle the section in terms of key, chords, tonic, subtonic, dominant chords, scales, modulations, and so forth. Why has the composer done this instead of doing something else? When the assumptions and the premises are accepted, all good music is logical (almost mathematically precise). If a composer has suddenly started nonsense when hitherto he has only had sense, ask why. It is possible that the music is faulty especially if it has been written by a modern composer.

Teacher White: That's funny. If the composer is an acknowledged master, then it is likely that you, Patten, are wrong. But right or wrong doesn't matter. What matters is that by analysis you have actively, not passively, interacted with the piece and to that extend, and for that reason, you have made part of the piece your own.

Student Patten: If you notice differences between you and the composer at a certain point, your analysis will become a personal matter and, for that matter, more easily remembered. Only a close analysis of each bar will be of any use. This is especially important where two sections appear to be almost identical. The pianist who misses the small subtleties of a composition may as well not play at all. Part of the critical spirit discussed above will get you to agree with what the composer has done or disagree with what he has done. If you agree, well and good. If you disagree, still better. Your disagreement with a section will enable you to all the more speedily recollect the section in question, as it will stand out in your memory because you disagreed.

About key: By analysis, memorize each change of key. Have the keys in mind. If everything else should fail, the keys may come to your assistance. If you know the cadences I-IV-V-I in that key, you can play those while desperately trying to figure out where and why your performance broke down.

O.K. That's the preliminaries. Are you ready to memorize *Für Elise*?

After diligent, focused, and intelligent listening, you should be able to know at all times exactly where the pianist is in the piece and you should be able to exactly predict exactly what comes next.

When you have reached that stage of facility, when you can easily identify A and B and A again and C and A at the end, then you are ready to begin your memory work by starting with an analysis of the piece and a division of the piece into identifiable patterns and structures.

Make a copy of the sheet music. Mark up the copy of the piece according to your analysis and then compare what you did to what we did. Don't mark up the original sheet music, just the copy. There is too much direct mark up in music instruction, a desecration of music. Your task is to condense what initially might appear to be a large, unorganized gaseous cloud of music into a number of small bite-size easily assimilated pellets (parts) that make sense to you.

DR. PATTEN'S INTELLECTUAL ANALYSIS OF *FÜR ELISE*

◆ ◆ ◆

Let's start by estimating the amount of time needed to get this piece into memory. Using the Fermi guesstimation, I think *Für Elise* will take at least five hours and not more than 20 hours. Taking the geometric mean of these two estimates we get (5 x 20 = 100; square root of 100 = 10) ten hours. Using the Patten guesstimation, we get 45 unique measures and a note density (estimated by eyeball method because I am too lazy to count the notes) of 10. Hence, 45 x 2 = 90 x 10 = 900 minutes or 15 hours. Rome wasn't built in a day. It took several centuries. *Für*

Elise will require 10 to 15 hours of devoted attention. This figure sounds right for me and includes time that I have already spent listening and doing research and doing analysis on the piece.

Your time to memory perfection may be more or less. It is a good idea to keep these figures in mind so that you don't get discouraged. When we get to different sections of the piece we will be able to do the same analysis to estimate the time needed to encode those sections. A reasonable appraisal of the time needed will help us schedule the amount of time needed. If *Für Elise* needs 10 hours and the best way of working on memory by the distributive rule is, more or less, 15 minutes a day, then I will need 40 days to learn to play the piece from memory. If 15 hours is needed, then 60 days would be more like it. Thus, if the recital is two months away, I should be able to do the job. If the recital is two weeks away, it is going to be difficult and I shall have to work about two hours a day or more, which is probably too much work.

What to Expect

Look at measures one and two and three:

Key

The key signature indicates C Major or its relative minor, A minor. Beethoven called this piece *Bagatelle in A Minor.* Therefore, the key is A minor. We can expect the notes of the A minor scale, the A minor chord (A-C-E), and the notes of A minor's relative major scale (C Major) and C Major's chord (C-E-G). Recall: C Major and A minor share the same pitches and have the same key signature.

Given A minor, we expect modulations to E Major, as E Major is the dominant, the fifth note up from A. Most of Western music is structured around this relationship: Tonic-Dominant. We may also expect modulations to D, as it is a fifth below A, making it the subdominant. F Major may come in because it is the subdominant of C Major, and G Major may appear as it is the dominant of C Major. E minor might also come in as it is the relative minor key of G. If we modulate to F Major, then we should expect some B-flat, as that is the subdominant of F Major. And if we get B-flat, then we might expect its relative minor key, which is G minor.

What to Do If You Are Lost

If, at this point, you are lost and have no idea what is involved here, then you had better start working on your music theory—the sooner, the better. If you do understand, now is the time to refresh your memory by playing the A minor scale, the C Major scale, the F Major scale, the D Major and D minor scales, the G Major scale, the G minor scale, and of course the E Major scale. It wouldn't hurt to also do the tonic, subdominant, and dominant cadences for each of these scales and to refresh your memory of the triads and their first and second inversions. A review of four-note structure would also help because Beethoven uses lots of seventh chords. He also likes sounding the top and bottom notes of a chord together. In his melodies, Beethoven often favors trichords (three-note combinations) and dichords (two-note combinations).

Meter

The indicated meter is 3/8, which means there are three beats to the measure, and each eighth note is worth one beat. Other versions of *Für Elise* in our collection use a 3/4 meter, where each quarter note is equal to one beat, but still with three beats per measure.

Dynamics

Pp means very soft—something most of us forget when we start to play this piece.

Will the Real *Für Elise* Please Stand Up?

After examining eight published versions of *Für Elise*, we find that no two versions exactly match. Which is the real *Bagatelle in A Minor*? Someday, someone (maybe us) will write a research paper on the different versions of *Für Elise*—the similarities, the differences, and why people believe their version is the one true and correct one. But not today. Today, our focus is how to put this piece into memory, how to look good while playing it, and how to have fun in the process.

Tempo

Moto grazioso means "very gracefully" and appears in a Beethoven sketch of this piece. Con moto (with movement) appears in some versions, though it's unclear whether this marking is in the original or added by editors. Many editions use poco moto (a little movement), probably from Ludwig Nohl, who presumably saw it on the original Beethoven autograph (now lost) that he discovered. Most pianists agree that the piece should be played with movement—that is, con moto. Some versions have no such instruction, nor do they have pedal markings. Since it's highly likely that any such markings are editorial and not original to Beethoven, let's not worry about them. After all, Beethoven is dead, and the dead, in case you haven't noticed, have little say over anything. It is we, the living, who bring the music to life.

Large Structure (refer to the sheet music that you should have downloaded free from the Forelise.com website).

Make two downloaded copies: one for you to study and mark up and the other as a clean reference sheet.

The large structure of the piece is in rondo form: ABACA. Section A has two themes. Section B follows and contrasts with A. The music then returns to A, then to C, and finally back to A as the finale. Hence, ABACA.

Examine your markup and get an idea of the divisions of the piece. If you agree with our markup, that's fine. If not, that's fine too. What you do for yourself is more important.

The Breakdown

Follow along as the markup is reviewed:

Section A starts at measure one and ends halfway through measure 25 at the cadence outlined by the black box labeled "CADENCE TO B." Section A consists of theme one (red line), theme one slightly modified (purple line), and theme two (green line).

Section B starts halfway through measure 25 (cadence in the black box) and ends at measure 39. Section B consists of two parts: B Hard (measures 26 to 32) and B Easy (measures 33 to 39).

A modified Section A (which we shall call A') then continues to measure 62, which introduces Section C. C ends at measure 84 (more or less). Section C consists of three parts: C1a (measures 62 to 69), C1b (measures 70 to 79), and C2 (measures 80 to 84).

Section A' comes back starting at measure 85 and continues to the end of the piece.

Look over the score and see if you agree with the division of the piece into the above sections. "Divide and conquer" is the strategy. Right now, we are at the "divide" part of the plan. Let's proceed to conquer.

The Strategy

Section B looks like the most difficult section of the piece. Why? Because it is.

Section C looks like the second most difficult because it is. Section A and its almost twin, Section A', look easy because of the repeats, the light note density, and the

PIANO BY HEART COMPANION

structured alternation of tonic and dominant arpeggios. Save Section A for last, as it looks the easiest.

Student Patten: The A section is the part most students want to learn and play. Me too. But I'm against just playing that part and nothing else. And I'm against simplified arrangements made for children. No shortened or simplified versions for me, please! Aim high. Aim for the real thing. Conquer B and C and play *Für Elise* in all its glory—play it in its complete form.

Attacking Section B

Section B consists of a hard part and an easier part. The hard part is introduced by the last three chords of measure 25, which look like a cadence from C7 to F and back to C7, as previously discussed.

ORELISE.COM

Play this cadence right now and get familiar with how it sounds and how your fingers look on the keys. Note how it seems to break up the routine of Section A and signals that something new is going to happen soon.

The new thing that follows is Section B1, seven unique measures with a note density of 11.5. Therefore, I estimate it will take 7 + 7 = 14 x 11.5 = 161 minutes, or about 23 minutes per measure, to get the hard part of B1 into my memory.

Perfection is the Enemy of Good

Remember that the calculations are based on achieving a perfect performance of the entire piece twice. However, you will likely reach an acceptable (though perhaps not perfect) rendition of the piece sooner. You'll probably achieve an almost-perfect rendition of the hard section of B1 before reaching the full 161-minute estimate.

We should aim for perfection, but we'll often achieve something less at first. Then, we'll aim again and achieve perfection sometimes. General George S. Patton once said, "A good plan today is better than a perfect plan tomorrow," meaning that good can, under the right circumstances, be better than perfect. Keep this in mind. The standards for music performance in the real world are quite different from those in the studio or concert hall. Often, good is good enough.

Start at the Beginning, Work Through the Middle, and Then Tackle the End Since the beginning of a section is so important as a lifesaver and an orientation point, start by attacking that first. It's hard to memorize more than two unique measures at a time due to the limitations of short-term memory, so focus only on Measure 25 to begin with. This cadence is a key lifesaver—a place to go if you break down, a reminder that you are starting a new section, and a wake-up call to your musicality.

So, memorize it now, memorize it once, and memorize it forever.

Measure 25:

On to measures 26 and 27, the true beginning of B1. To get a better handle on the memory of these two measures, give them labels. Measure 25 is the transition or cadence to part B and introduction to the new key of F, which is the bass of measure 26.

The seven measures that follow the introduction to B will be called measure B1 (measure 26) measure B2 (measure 27), B3, B4 and so forth up to B7 which concludes hard B. These names work for me so I have placed them on my mark up sheet.

What Works for You?

What works for you is what you should use. You might want to use colors starting with red (that could be measure 26, what I called measure B1), orange (27), yellow (28), green (29), blue (30), indigo (31), and violet (32).

Notice that I kept things organized according to the progression of colors in the rainbow. If I need to recall that order we can use a mnemonic device like ROY G. BIV where each letter of that name will recall a color of the rainbow. R = red, O = orange, and Y = yellow, G = green, B = blue, I = indigo, V = violet.

Note about B7. Some versions have a turn in the middle of B7. Ask your teacher about this. Most would play the C and then play the turn (DCBC) with the second E in the bass. Omission of the turn is OK, too, and will not distract from the beauty of the measure. Although, frankly, I think the measure does sound better and more interesting and is better able to introduce B2 with the turn than without it. Choose!

By now you should be able to think up some of your own hooks and memory tricks. Such hooks and pegs will help get the hard B section in your memory. When you have it in your memory, you will then be able to forget it because your visual, motor, and auditory recall will function automatically, and you won't need the pegs or memory hooks. But for the moment, you might try to use associations, preferably your own associations, and not what is printed in this book. You have to learn to crawl before you can walk. You have to learn to walk before you can water ski. You should learn to ice skate before you luge. You have to learn to make your own associations before you can memorize with ease. And don't forget narrative, narrative, narrative. Try to think of some narratives to help.

PROGRAM MUSIC

◆ ◆ ◆

Sometimes, the music will suggest the narrative, as in the 1812 Overture, where you have no trouble figuring out who is attacking whom and at what time by listening for the French and Russian national anthems. In song pieces, follow the words of the song and sing along to get the associations needed to recall the music. If a song-like piece doesn't have words, make them up. Even if the words are silly, if they help, use them.

Student Patten: Making up words and singing them to myself as I play helped me memorize Schumann's *Happy Farmer*.

Occasionally, the composer will give you the narrative explicitly as Scott Joplin did in his *Crush Collision March* (registered for copyright October 15, 1896), with its dedication to the M.K.&T railroad (known to most as the Katy railroad). The Crush Collision was a head-on crash and destruction of two locomotives on September 15, 1896. The idea was that two trains should hit each other head-on at 60 miles an hour. William Crush intended the crash as a public relations device, but it also was an entertainment, which drew a crowd of over 50,000 people each of whom paid 25 cents admission to watch the crash. The firemen and the engineers jumped clear before the crash, but the boilers exploded on impact, killing three spectators and injuring dozens of others. Scott Joplin was there and programmed the march describing the crash. Details of the music may be found in Edward A. Berlin's excellent book (see bibliography). As far as the music score is concerned, the collision occurs in the interlude within the trio section, with a description written by Joplin right into the printed score:

"The noise of the trains while running at the rate of sixty miles per hour,
Whistling for the crossing,
Noise of the trains
Whistle before the collision
The collision"

The roar of the trains is represented by a chromatic bass, which gets lower as the trains near. The train whistles are high-pitched, tuned a major second apart, each with accompanying grace notes, and they get higher as the trains get closer. The work shows Joplin's interest in dramatic depiction and the narrative focus is supplied for you to help you know what's happening when. Such a narrative would help encode that piece in the memory.

We don't have such a narrative for *Für Elise*. So what are we to do?

Stop and think. What do we do if the composer has not supplied a narrative to help us memorize his work? What do we do when we don't know what to do?

Answer: When we don't know what to do, we analyze the situation and act accordingly. In this case, we make up a narrative to trigger memory associations and help us get the music in our memory. We add the narrative to the other tricks we will use to help encode the piece. Remember, multiple associations do not impair memory. Multiple associations augment and improve memory. You should have no hesitation in using whatever associations come to mind and keeping those that seem to help. Thus, you could use a number-based (that is numeric) set of labels, plus a color-based set of labels, plus an alphabet-based set of labels (that is abecedarian), plus a crazy narrative, plus an analytical narrative based on key changes, one, some, all, or any combination of associations and ideas. But remember: You have to do it. That's what we said: YOU. You have to make up your own mnemonic system for this piece. Our suggestions are just suggestions.

In a recent classical concert on board the Cunard ship Queen Victoria, pianist Ray Alston announced that Debussy's *Clair de Lune* is about a couple dancing in the moonlight and that Debussy was "painting an impressionist painting" about this couple. Have you any doubt about what visual and narrative mnemonic tricks Ray Alston uses to recall this piece as he plays it? Whether he is correct or not does not matter. What counts, what really matters, is that that image and that narrative works for him and enabled him to play the piece from memory and play it well.

Side Bar About Labels Hard and Easy

There are positives and negatives to labels. Hard will alert us to concentrate our attention on that part of the piece. But Hard may also prejudice our performance. If we think it is hard, then our subconscious mind might actually foul us up by believing the label. Call something Easy – ditto the reverse.

Divide and Conquer B

Next we need to divide the intro to part B (measure 25) into something our minds can easily grasp. The intro has two parts. Part one is the A minor (AEA) arpeggio set that is old hat from the sight reading experience with this piece. A is the tonic for this piece and E is the subdominant, so the relation is easy to remember.

The second part of introduction to B consists of three sixteenth chords and is a C7-F-C7 cadence. By focusing directly on the measure, put the exact formation of the cadence into your visual memory. Furthermore, remind yourself with an intellectual analysis by telling yourself the first C7 is B flat C in bass, EC in Treble, with the EC a sixth apart. F (the IV chord of C Major; also known as the subdominant) is represented by AC in bass and FC above, with the FC a perfect 5th apart, and then we go back to C7, this time with one more note added above and below. The note added above is a G, and the note added below is a G, so that shouldn't be difficult to recall. Beethoven made these chords staccato, according to some versions – another head up and wake-up to introduce a new musical set of ideas to follow. By the way, CFC suggests what the next item to follow is. CFC suggests F, and F major is exactly what we get next.

Did you notice that the text is repeating itself?

Repetition is good. Repetition cements the memory. We should not despise repetition. We should embrace it. The soul and science of memory is intelligent repetition.

The last upper chord in this measure is first inversion C. That idea may also help me recall the chord. By placing your hands on the keys and noting with your eyes the positions needed to play measure 25, you help fix the music in your visual memory. By hearing yourself play this measure, you help fix the music in your aural (ear) memory. By moving your fingers from the AEA arpeggio to the C7 F C7 cadence, you help fix the music in your motor memory, which will include the sequence of notes that leads to the cadence. By repeating the actions many times (suggestion: at least ten correct repeats), you transfer the memory from stage one to stage two and on to stage three memory.

Tricks and Tips

Practice the intro measure 25 until it comes automatically until your fingers get it,, as well as your intellect, gets it. Then try to forget it. You can't. Also, the feeling of accomplishment you get when you automatically play this introduction to the next section. Most people smile when they finally get this measure correct, and others even laugh out loud. How about you?

Intro to B Is Now in the Memory

Wow! The cadences were easy. Don't bang them out. Don't rush them.

Student Patten: I like to play the cadence chords louder than expected so that those listeners who are alert will know that a new section in a different key has arrived. I also like to play them louder so that those listeners who are not alert will get alert, and I like to play them louder so those who have fallen asleep will wake up and know that a new section has arrived.

Memorizing measure 25 took me less than five minutes. How about you? How long did it take you to memorize measure 25?

(Look now at measure 26, which I called B1, and color it red in your mind's eye)

B1 looks difficult, and so does B2, B3, and so forth. Therefore, we need to dream up or imagine some chunking tools, or we need to recognize a pattern in the measures that we can hang some memories on. The keys are going to help as the modulations seem reasonable and expectable. The regular pattern of six notes in the bass is going to be a great memory peg because recognized patterns help organize memory.

Before you tackle B1, you might try to memorize the bass pattern. It also helps to recognize that most of the measures have an Alberti bass and the measures that do not have this form of familiar but nowadays little-esteemed formula of arpeggio accompaniment will stand out for the reason that they are different.

Teacher White: Little esteemed? Where did that idea come from? The Alberti bass is well esteemed by many, and students would do well to learn it.

Thus, looking over the measures (and visualizing them in the mind's eye) try to construct this image as a chart to memorize:

PIANO BY HEART COMPANION

B1 (red, measure 26) is in F major with the chord in root position. So, I'll play the bass Alberti style: FACACA. While I'm focused on B1, why not memorize it right now? The trick is to connect the treble notes to the bass pattern. Play a fast F major chord in the treble with the first F in the bass, then hold the last note of the F chord in the treble (which is C, of course) until your left hand catches up and plays FACA. Now, play F in the treble with C in the bass and finish the bass with the A. Right after that, descend by one note and hit E with your right-hand finger. Cool!

Work on this measure for a while to get the feel of it. It's actually pretty easy once you understand the pattern and rhythm. The rhythm is important because it's repeated in the next measure. Now, play the introduction to B (measure 25), followed by measure 26 (B1). Repeat it until you get it right and feel comfortable playing without hesitation. To remember that you need to hit F when C comes around in the bass, just recall that F and C are related as they form the F major chord, which is the key of this measure. C is the dominant of F.

Holy cow! We can now play two measures of B hard: the intro and B1. That means we're 25% finished with B hard!

B2 (orange, measure 27) is in B-flat major (the subdominant of F), with F kept as a common tone, maintaining the same voice position and putting the B-flat chord in the second inversion. So, I'll play F B-flat D B-flat D B-flat as the Alberti bass. Practice this a few times to get the feel of moving from FACAC to F B-flat D B-flat D B-flat. Remember, in Alberti bass, the middle and end tones are repeated, so there are six notes to play.

How to Remember Measure B2 Is in B-flat: Find a System That Works for You

Student Patten: For me, I imagine a giant orange descending from the sky and crushing a bee until it's flat. (Only kidding!) In reality, I remind myself that F major goes to its subdominant chord, which is B-flat major. This narrative works for me. What works for you?

Now that you're focused on measure B2, why not memorize it here and now? The trick is to match the treble notes to what we know must be played in the bass. With F in the bass, repeat the last note of the previous measure (E). Why do E and F go together? Well, that's a long story, but it likely stems from our expectations derived from Western music. E leads naturally into F going up the scale, and F leads into E when descending. The reasoning, though, doesn't matter much as long as it helps!

PIANO BY HEART COMPANION

We've already sounded E, and we just need to sound it again with F in the bass to get going. Play out the Alberti bass with B-flat and then D. With D in the bass, play D in the treble (D pairs with D), then return to B-flat in the bass and hit D again. This time, play the upper B-flat with the bass D, then hit B-flat one last time in this measure. Follow with A in the treble, dropping a half step to sound a lonely A, similar to how we sounded the lonely E in the previous measure. (Notice the interesting relationship between A and E again—perhaps not just a coincidence?)

And there you have it, B2!

Play B2 a few times. It sounds fantastic! Now, play the intro (measure 25), then measure 26, and finally measure 27. Recognize the sequence: Cadence, F in the bass, then B-flat in the bass. Practice these three measures until they sound and feel right.

Take a break—you've just achieved something great! Not many people in the world can do what you've just done. You're special. You might even be the only person on your block who can play these measures from memory. Bask in the light of your achievement and enjoy the moment!

Student Patten: It's important to reward yourself, especially when others might not. When teachers don't reward you for your progress, reward yourself—right?

Teacher White: Patten, you really are something else!

WELCOME BACK FROM YOUR BREAK!

◆ ◆ ◆

B3 (yellow, measure 28) is F, E, G minor 7th, E, G minor 7th, E. This combination stands out because it's different in the way it looks, feels, and sounds. We could consider the bass as a sort of Alberti pattern if that helps memory or view the F-G-B-flat as part of a C7 chord. Given that it's a C7, we might expect to move to F major, similar to the sequence we saw in the introduction to section B1. I like this idea because it reinforces the memory connection.

Teacher White: But F isn't part of C7. How do you explain that?

PIANO BY HEART COMPANION

Student Patten: It's a pedal tone, or we could say it introduces C7. Whether or not it's true doesn't matter as long as it helps me remember. What's important is that the sequence is F-E, F-G-B-flat, E, F-G-B-flat, E.

Since the bass part in B3 is unusual, I'll give it a special label: the nice-sounding bass (instead of "weird"). It has three E's (in positions 2, 4, and 6), which can be a helpful memory tool, and each E lands on the second note of each major beat in the measure. Another chunking tool: F-E, followed by F plus some other notes (G & B-flat, forming a G minor chord), then E again, then the same F plus the same notes, then E once more.

B3 will be easy to recall because of its uniqueness in both form and musical substance. The treble part will also aid memory: It starts at A (with F in the bass), then moves down one note at a time:

A pairs with F in the bass
G pairs with E
F pairs with G minor (or C7)
E pairs with E in the bass
D pairs with G minor
C pairs with E

The treble in B3 is simply A-G-F-E-D-C. Pretty straightforward! Learning to play this from memory is easier if you first master the bass and then attach the descending scale to it. Play it ten times for reinforcement.

Easy, right? If not, take a break and come back when your mind is fresh. If it still feels difficult, assess your progress after a good night's sleep.

Onward!

What note should come next as we continue the descent down the scale into the next measure? B-flat, of course, because we already know that B4 is in F major, and the next note down from C in the descending scale is B-flat. I suggest playing B-flat with the second finger of the right hand, then A with the thumb, and then B-flat with the third finger, leaving enough fingers to play the nice A-G-A-B-flat sequence to end the measure.

Tips and Tricks: Play this measure over a few times—it has a luscious tone quality that's unforgettable. When played correctly, it will always be recognized as great music. Holy cow! Now we've learned four more measures of B Hard, meaning we're more than halfway through!

On to B4: B4 (green, measure 29) starts with F in the bass and the F chord in root position, as we already know. So play FACACA. This is the same as the bass in B1. Therefore, another memory tool is: B1 bass = B4.

On to B5: B5 (blue, measure 30) also starts with F in root position, so play FACACA. This is the same as B1 and B4. Now that we are at B4 and B5, how about memorizing them?

The bass is easy: FACACA. B4 (measure 29) has an interesting turn in the treble that shouldn't be too difficult if we follow the rules of memory. We already know that the treble in measure 29 starts with B-flat, as it's the natural note to follow the long descent in unique measure 28. So, sound F in the bass with B-flat in the treble. Continuing the descent, sound A with C in the bass, and get ready for the turn.

The turn is entirely on beat three of the measure and starts by sounding B-flat with C. The right hand then executes the turn by going down to A, then G, and back to A (which is sounded with A in the bass), and finally back to B-flat, this time alone.

That was fast! But if you stay alert and see the pattern, it shouldn't cause too many headaches. The good news is that the turn sets up the next measure nicely: FACACA again in the bass, but an easier treble, with C held for two beats, and then on the third beat, play D followed by D# (B5, measure 30, outlined in blue).

On the other hand, this could be a misprint. I play the treble D with A in the bass and then add the D#. This sounds better and matches the patterns of some other B1 measures. But if you prefer to play the treble D with C in the bass and then D# with A, go ahead—both options sound good.

OK, great! Let's review: Now that we have some association handles on the measures, we can let go of the colors and link our memories with more relevant associations:

Intro: This is the intro to the section—AEA in A minor followed by the cadence. This measure is unique and hard to forget.

B1: The FAC Alberti bass with the upper F hit with the last C, followed by E.

B2: Switches to F-B-flat-D Alberti, with E sounded with bass F, then right hand sounding D, then upper B-flat with D. After the remaining left-hand B-flat, the upper A sounds alone.

B3: The descent with F-E-F-E-F-E in the bass, except the last two F's have that G minor flavor.

B4: The turn measure. The bass is FACACA again. Practice the turn from the notes until you get it—it isn't hard. Start the measure with B-flat hit with F, descend to A, and hit C in the bass. The turn itself starts with B-flat—you'll see it on the sheet. B5: Leads into the key change that ends section B and prepares us for B6.

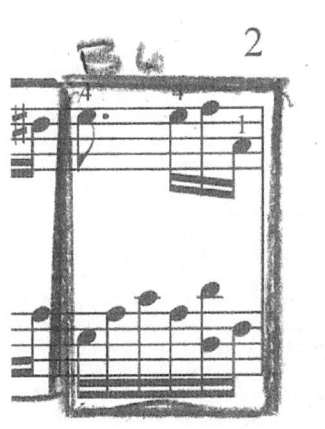

B6 (indigo, measure 31) divides itself into two parts – the first four notes are A minor in the second inversion (EACA) and the next two notes are D minor in the root position but played DD in bass with F in treble. My mnemonic for this measure will be B6AmDm (colored indigo). Heck, it might be just as easy to memorize that the last two notes are DD in the bass with the F above followed by F in bass and A above. You might tell yourself F and A go together because they are the first and third notes of the F major chord.

PIANO BY HEART COMPANION

Play this to get a feel for it. It is much easier to visualize and play than it is to talk about. Notice how F in bass and A in treble leads right into G in bass and C in treble. What about the relation of C and G might help you remember their combination here?

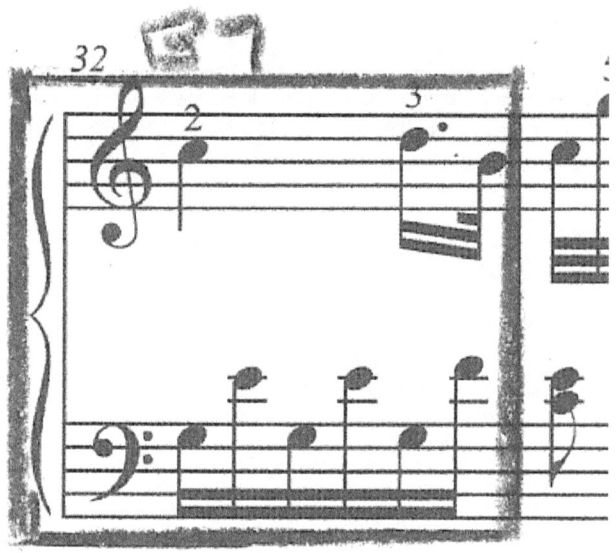

B7 (violet, measure 32; violet = the end of the rainbow and the end of hard section B) is in C Major (G on the bottom and C on top). That is the beginning of the GE GE GF: GE GE (the famous electronic company) followed by GF (two GE refrigerators worked, but the third failed, and hence the third G gets an F). Shout this combination out loud to help you fix the memory.

BERNARD M. PATTEN

REVIEW TIME IS NEVER WASTED

◆ ◆ ◆

Review the list of B measures 1 to 7 and then recite it from memory. Notice how the organizational scheme of intro followed by numbered measures helps recall. If you miss some items, go back and review and try to discover why that happened. Discover the obstacles, as that is the necessary step toward overcoming them. Now augment the intellectual associations by playing B hard with your left hand. Play it several times to get the motor memory down. Look for errors and correct them. Get the vision of your hands and the positions on the keys. Anything that helps remind you will help remind you.

Test yourself by using some system to randomly recall the numbers 1 to 7. Flashcards will do this for you.

Student Patten: As for me, I like to roll dice. If a number 1 to 7 comes up, I shout what the bass is for that number in section B that we have just studied. Testing yourself is an excellent way to make sure you really know something cold. Shout out the answers. There is a tremendous difference between thinking you know something and actually proving you know it.

Another Possible Way

Or you can test yourself by the questions:
What's the intro to B?
What's the bass for B1? B2? B3? B4? B5? B6? And B7?

When you can play the accompaniment and shout it out loud, give yourself a small reward. But notice you still can't play B. You have to now study each measure and hang the treble notes onto the bass. That is what is going to make hard B hard or easier than you think, depending on whether or not you start to apply some of the memory tricks.

Attaching the treble to the bass notes in hard part B – more associations – Remember the mind benefits from, and does not suffer from, multiple associations and approaches. And (we repeat) review time is never wasted, as repetition is the soul and science of memory. Repetition is the soul of memory because neurons must be fired together in order for them to wire together.

Let's start by attaching B1 to the intro.

B1 (red, measure 26) looks easy. Picture in your mind's eye a large B, a large 1F, and color them, the B, the 1, and the F, blood red. That will remind you that the bass of B1 is the F chord. In this measure, in treble, the right hand plays a fast F chord while the left hand plays the initial F. The right hand holds the C (the end note of the fast F chord) while the left does its thing, catching up by playing the Alberti bass FACA. When the bass gets to C again, the right hand hits an F in treble. How can we remember that? It's up to you. You have to construct an association. As for us, we know Beethoven likes to relate the end notes of chords. So, if the bass is a C, and the key is F, the chance is good that the treble note will be an F, which is the other end of the FAC chord from C.

And wow! Not incidentally, that is exactly what we find in this measure: C in bass sounded with F in treble. From there, we continue with the Alberti, completing it with the A, and then the treble sounds a short E, one note below the F that we just played. Presto! We are on our way to having B1 in memory. Play this a few times, getting a real feeling for the rhythm, as the same rhythm is repeated in measure B2 and B7.

Now play the intro and B1 several times to put it in motor memory. Give this power of performance. Make them sit up and pay attention.

Student Patten: By the way, I have heard Van Cliburn sometimes play the two small notes of B1 as grace notes. Not me. I play them fast with the F in the bass and hold the C until I am ready to hit the top F with the C in the Alberti bass. I think it sounds better, but some teachers say differently and play those notes their way. And that's OK.

Another way is to just duplicate the F chord in bass and treble. That sounds pretty good, but most would consider it unofficial and not recommended.

Take a short break before attacking B2, B3, and B4 (again).

Review and play again the bass of B1, B2, B3, and B4. By now, you should know the bass of these measures by their chords: F, B flat, yellow special with the three E's and G minor combo, F, and F.

Now concentrate on the pattern in treble. B2 has E on beat one, then D (same tone in bass) on beat two, and then the spectacular high B flat (also sounded with D) followed by a short A in treble. Play this as your aural memory is going to help here. Treble in B3 is descending notes in order starting with a repeated A. Hence, B4 treble is AGFEDC. B5 continues the descent to B flat and then A with the B flat on beat one and the A on beat two. And then, for a special treat, the unexpected arrives—a turn with B flat sounded with C on beat three, then down AG and up again AB. Sound the treble A with the A in the bass.

B5 looks similar to and different from B1. The two measures both have the Alberti bass F chord, with beat three in B5 having a D followed by a D#. The similarities and the difference should make B5 easy. B1 and B5 are the same, except the last two notes are FE in B1 and DD# in B5, with the rhythm in B1 slightly different from B5.

The Lifesavers of Section B

Now focus on B6 and B7. Those two measures are important because they are the lifesavers that you can go to if you get fouled up in B hard. Knowing B6 and B7 cold will give you confidence that you can always get through B hard looking OK, and you will be able to get from B hard to B easy (the cadenza part of B) easily.

Recall we already know the bass of both these measures: AmDm for B6 and GEGEGF for B7. So, what do we put on top of the second inversion A minor? Answer: nothing much. The first treble note is E played with E in the bass. E is then played again, this time with the A (note four). Then, as we know already, D is played in the bass (many manuscripts, including the original, have two D's an octave apart), so we should expect the treble note to be F (van B. likes thirds, no matter how far apart), which it is. Then the F is played in the bass, and we should expect, by the major third rule, that the treble will be A, which it is. This nice sequence should be easy to recall.

On to B7, where we know the bass is GEGEGF: The first bass note is G, so the top note should be C, the other end of the C major chord, which it is. Then, there is nothing in the treble on beat two, and then we get to bass note four, which is C. Sounded with C is a nice turn: DCBC, and back to D, which is sounded with the G that begins beat three of the measure—another example of the end note rule, as G major is GBD. The bass F follows, and then a short B. The four notes of beat three are, of course, part of G7 (GDFB). You already know the bass is GF, so the remaining notes of G7 have to be D and B in the treble.

If you don't understand this, don't worry about it. Just memorize the configuration, the way it sounds at the piano, and the way it looks when you have your hands in position. You shouldn't have much trouble. And if you do have trouble, don't worry. Hundreds of students have spent hundreds of hours learning this part of the piece, and they have eventually succeeded. You will too. But we want to emphasize here that it is important to work out these problems in your head and on the piano. Think about them, not just read what we have written about them. In fact, you will benefit more by doing the analysis yourself and making your own associations.

Your job as a memory musician is to go through and work through the steps yourself, even out loud, and in real time at the piano to help reinforce your thoughts and your memory.

PIANO BY HEART COMPANION

Other Versions

Some versions of the piece have a turn in B7, but the turn in B7 is not in the original manuscript, so you can leave it out if you wish. If you do leave it out, that makes B7 really easy: it's GE GE GF, playing C with the first G and D with the third G. F follows in bass, and the B is tacked on leading into the C's in the next measure. Recall, B is the lead tone to C, so this makes sense.

OK?

Play measures B5, B6, and B7 until motor memory has them down. And review the intro, B1, B2, B3, and B4. We are almost there.

Take a short break before playing the whole thing.

Now go back and play the intro and the entire hard B as many times as you need to in order to fix the memory. Once you have learned B hard, keep it in your memory by replaying it to test or refresh your memory—or both. Review time is never wasted.

Now that you know B hard, make sure you review it several times a day. Remember the distributive rule: multiple short sessions are much, much better than one long session. You worked hard to learn it, and you need to work hard to keep it in the memory. The frequent repetitions will also give you a chance to polish the style and vary the dynamics to see how this piece should be (according to your feelings) played. How long does it take to play hard B anyway? Answer: merely seconds.

Next, it is time to coast because B easy is a lot easier than B hard. In fact, I would say that if you have mastered B hard, you are more than halfway to mastering *Für Elise*.

Let's tackle B easy, which starts at measure 33 in your copy of *Für Elise*.

B easy is a cadenza that has five unique measures and a note density of 13. It should take me 5 + 5 = 10 x 13 = 130 minutes to play it perfectly.

Looking it over, I see some nice patterns, so I am going to avoid key and note chunking and try to use pattern chunking to get this part in the memory.

THE PROFOUND ADVANTAGE OF PATTERN RECOGNITION

◆◆◆

In music, math, and most parts of life, you are way ahead if you recognize and use a pattern because pattern recognition reflects an immediacy of perception. For example: What's 34 x 11? Some may find that multiplication difficult unless they know that anything times 11 can be done by adding the digits and inserting the number between the first and last digit. Thus, 34 x 11 is 374 because 3 + 4 = 7, and inserting 7 between 3 and 4 gives 374. Similarly, 234 x 11 is 2574 because 2 + 3 = 5 and 3 + 4 = 7, so inserting 57 gives 2574.

More on the Advantages of Pattern Recognition

Take the case of Carl Friedrich Gauss (1777–1855). As a ten-year-old, he was given this problem by his teacher:

What is the sum of the numbers from 1 to 100?

While Gauss's classmates were busy adding the numbers one by one, Gauss saw the pattern. If the numbers from one to fifty are lined up left to right and the numbers 100 to 51 are lined up under them left to right, then each column adds to 101 (e.g., on the extreme right, 50 + 51 = 101, and on the extreme left, 1 + 100 = 101, and so on for every column in between). This pattern recognition leads to the idea that the sum of numbers 1 to 100 is 101 x 50 columns, which equals 5050. Gauss had the answer way ahead of the other kids in his class and, more importantly, was sure he didn't make a silly addition error in the process, a problem that probably afflicted those who did the problem the hard way. Using the same system, you can add all the numbers from one to 20 in a small amount of time. Try this—you will like it!

With the idea of pattern recognition in mind, let's attack B easy.

BERNARD M. PATTEN

The Pattern of B Easy

The right-hand pattern is CG, then down an octave to play G with the upper G. The pattern is then simply to go up one note with the thumb and keep hitting the high G after. Hence, CGGGAGBGCGDG (twelve notes—twice what we are used to per measure as these are thirty-second notes, not sixteenth notes). The kids I've heard play this love it because they can play it fast without much thought. Me too.

With the first C in treble is CE in bass, kind of a half-baked C Major chord. Then nothing much happens in the bass until B is sounded in treble. At that point, play a small G7 in lower treble (FG). When C is sounded in upper treble, complete the C triad by sounding EG in low treble. When D is sounded in higher treble, play the G7 again in lower treble, this time adding a D. Very cool and very logical if you understand your chords. If you don't understand the chords, the memory task will be 500 times harder.

The number of words needed to discuss this simple pattern is far more than is needed to memorize the pattern by touch and sound. It is sort of like trying to tell someone how to ride a bicycle. It is much more difficult to talk about it than it is to actually do it.

So play this measure without much study, relying on sound, motor memory, and pattern recognition, forgetting about chords and notes.

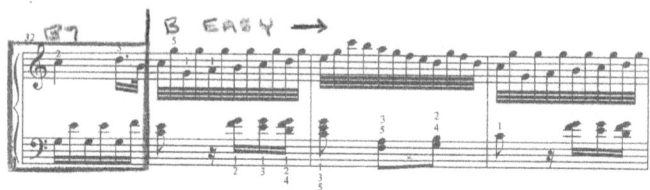

In measure two of B easy (measure 34 in your copy), the pattern is even easier. Beat one is in C Major in bass with E on top, beat two is in the subdominant of C Major, which is F with A on top, and beat three is in G, which is the dominant of C Major with D on top. Measure two of B easy starts with the expected EG in higher treble with a root C Major in the lower treble, then jumps to G and then (where else?) to a higher C. The key is C, so if you have played EG as part of the C Major arpeggio, you need to complete the triad of C Major. C then steps down to B. The step to B reminds me that the next key is F, so I will descend by single notes starting with A (and sounding FA in bass). Hence, AGFE while holding FA in bass. The next note in the sequence and the beginning of beat three should be D, reminding me of the key of G, so I shall play GB in bass while playing D in treble to complete the G chord. Beat three is a little tricky to think about but easy to hear and play, DGFD, which leads right into a two-measure exact repeat, except instead of playing CE in the bass as we did with the first measure of B hard, we only play C (red circle).

This is a simplification and a violation of the usual rule, but what can we do? Sometimes Beethoven likes to trick us, as do all good composers. These two measures use nice classical modulations in major scales, so they should sound happy and bright, which incidentally they do, especially when played fast and loud.

OK, great! We should have the first four measures of the cadenza in tow. Practice these until you can play them confidently without reference to notes. By the way, what is a cadenza? Answer: A cadenza is a sequence of notes or chords comprising the close of a musical phrase and often signals that a new musical idea is coming.

Student Patten: It took me only ten minutes to master this after my initial analysis. In fact, it took me way longer to write about it (and read what I wrote about it) than it took to memorize it. How about you? You might do it quicker or slower. No matter. The idea is to do it.

The last two measures of B easy are easy and identical and consist of long E (one and a half beats), followed by the sequence BED#.

Play that sequence over a few times. It should remind you of the beginning of *Für Elise*. Sure enough, it leads right into section A, which is the beginning. That leaves measure six of B easy, which has as beats two and three the same sequence of notes as the two measures that follow, which is EBED#.

That leaves only one beat of measure six of B easy to memorize, and that is E major (E in treble and G#B in bass), and then F in treble with the last two notes of beat one identical to the last two notes of beats two and three (ED#). Review the entire B easy and play it until you can do it well. Then patch it onto B hard, and you will have mastered the hardest part of *Für Elise*. Next, we will do the next hardest part, section C. After that, it's smooth flying.

ATTACKING C BY DIVIDE AND CONQUER

◆ ◆ ◆

Fasten your seat belts. Make sure your seats are upright, and your tray table is in the stowed position. Turn off cell phones and other electronic devices. Put your carry-on bag under the seat in front of you. Ready for take-off? We are in for some rough turbulence before we return to smooth air. Section C is difficult, but not as difficult as section B hard.

Divide and Conquer Section C

Section C starts at measure 62 with an A in treble for one beat and a drone of six As in the bass.

BERNARD M. PATTEN

Section C consists of two parts: a hard part and an easy cadenza, which introduces C2. The hard part can be divided into two similar yet different parts, each running eight measures. Then there appear two measures that announce the arrival of C2. These two measures are our old friends, I V, A minor (the I) – two beats and pause for one beat, followed by the E major (the V) – one beat and pause for two beats. Memorize this cadenza. If you need it, it can be a lifesaver during your next performance.

Let's start with the first part of section C and name it. Call it what you wish. For us, it is C1a. The almost identical eight measures that follow C1a we call C1b. After C1b, there is a two-measure bridge to the easy part of section C, which starts at measure 80. That easy section of C we shall call C2.

Notice the names are easy to remember because they reflect our actual mental organization of the piece and they are similar to the actual organization of the piece. Test your understanding now by closing your eyes and naming the parts of section C.

PIANO BY HEART COMPANION

Did you get C1a, C1b, and C2? Or did you get C1a, C1b, Bridge, C2? If not, reread the above paragraph and study the score. C2 also has two parts, one three measures long, and the other two measures long. The first part is arpeggios of A minor played as triplets, headed up with some nice trichords (DCB) headed down.

© 2006 - 2008 FORELISE.COM

The second part of C2 is a chromatic scale headed down to the repeat of section A. Accordingly, I call these two parts of C2 A minor arpeggios and C2 chromatic.

Thus we have a mental map of C:
C1a
C1b
Bridge
C2 A minor arpeggios mixed with trichord descents
C2 chromatic descents

C2 looks like a good lifesaver so I will study it first. The bridge is simple:

BERNARD M. PATTEN

One A minor chord (measure 78 in your copy) is followed by E Major (EG# in bass; EB in treble). The A minor (in first inversion) is held for two beats, and the E Major is held for one beat, followed by two beats of silence. The silence is important as it signals a transition to a new musical idea. Mozart believed that silences are just as important as the sounded notes, so let's pay attention to and respect the silences.

Put your hands in position and memorize these two lifesaving measures. This is where you may go if you foul up in C1a or break down in C1b. This is your lifesaver, so memorize it well. Name it the transition, the bridge, or whatever seems memorable to you.

Student Patten: For me, it's a cadence, so that's what I call it, and I recall it as the cadence that introduces A minor triplet arpeggios.

Use your visual memory of the printed notes and the visual memory of the position of your hands on the keyboard. Say the names of the chords out loud as you play them. Right after the two-beat silence of the bridge's second measure, the cadenza starts with a very low A and a low A.

The pattern is two ascending A minor arpeggio triplets followed by a descending trichord of DCB. The root triad A minor is struck with the D of beat three and held for the duration of the measure — that is, the A minor chord is held for one beat. In fact, every time A minor is sounded, it is held for one beat. The next measure is the same, except it starts an octave higher and with the A minor sounded at the beginning of beat one and beat three. The next measure repeats the pattern of measure two an octave higher. The patterns are clear-cut, and you should be able to master these three measures without tears.

The chromatic section begins with the A minor in the bass and a B flat above. The bass is silent after beat one, and the chromatic scale descends (one semitone at a time) in triplets (but sounded equally) over the last two measures of section C, heading into the start of section A. Some pianists play the chromatic section as a scale and not as triplets, while others play it so fast that you can't tell whether it is a scale or triplets. I play it as a scale because that's what it is, even though it appears to be written in triplets.

Student Patten: No, change that. My preference depends on how I feel. Sometimes triplets sound right, and I use just three fingers to play each triplet, 4/3/2. Other times, I play it as a chromatic scale. It all depends on how my feelings flow, and who can really explain how one's feelings flow? As a chromatic scale, I play with fingers 3/1 until I get to two white notes, and then it's 3/2/1 followed by 3/1. Check this out with your teacher and play what works best for you.

Have fun playing this chromatic descent. Played right, it's impressive. If you don't know the fingers for the descent, ask your teacher. When I'm in my chromatic mood, I like to start my fourth finger of my right hand on the B flat and play fingers 4/3/2/1, then 3/2/1, 3/1, 3/2/1, etc., eventually landing with my fourth finger on that E of the first measure of section A (measure 85 in this part of *Für Elise*). Once there, it's just a matter of playing part A again.

Teacher White: This is not normal chromatic fingering. Normal is 3/1 until two white notes, when it's 3/2/1.

Student Patten: Sometimes, when I'm in a certain (weird) mood, though, as mentioned, I will play the chromatic descent as triplets using finger 4/3/2 all the way down. The effect is interesting and different. Sometimes I play it with the fingering suggested by Jimmy.

Divide and Conquer C1a and C1b

Hard C1a starts at measure 62 in your copy and ends at measure 69; C1b starts at measure 70 and ends at measure 77. Thus, C1a runs eight measures, and so does C1b.

PIANO BY HEART COMPANION

In the last measure of C1a (measure 69), the bass plays FEFE, while in the last measure of C1b (measure 77), the bass plays FEDE. This slight difference in the rhythm of the bass provides a clue to help distinguish between the two sections and aids memory recall.

Idea #3: Both C1a and C1b start in A minor. The bass drones on A for three measures while the treble sounds A minor arpeggios and then moves to other variations.

Idea #4: There are triplet arpeggios in both C1a and C1b, which makes both sections rhythmically similar and easier to grasp once you get the feel for the pattern.

Idea #5: The treble melodies in C1a and C1b are different in terms of pitch movement. In C1a, there is more repetition of the same notes, while in C1b, the treble line ascends with a different set of pitches, adding contrast between the two.

Teacher White: Good job, Patten. You've found several significant memory hooks that can help you remember and play this section of *Für Elise*. The use of repeated rhythm in the bass and the differences in the treble lines are strong cues for memorization. Keep practicing with these in mind.

Student Patten: Thanks! Now that I've got these ideas down, the section doesn't seem so difficult anymore. By identifying those small but significant differences, I think I'll be able to recall C1a and C1b more easily.

Teacher White: Excellent! Let's keep this momentum going and move on to the next part when you're ready. Don't forget to play these sections repeatedly to lock them into your muscle memory.

There are treble notes at beat one, two, and three (see above), whereas in the last measure of C1b there are treble notes at beat one and beat three:

Idea #3

The bass of C1a and C1b looks pretty organized and simple, so I can use it as a memory peg. C1a bass has the first five measures with only an A, which is sounded six times in each measure. Sounding the same note in a measure I will call a drone, and if I can count to six, I can keep track of where I am at all times.

PIANO BY HEART COMPANION

Thus, C1a has five measures of drone.

C1b has almost the same bass for the first four measures, except the first measure of C1b (measure 70 in your copy) has two A's an octave apart. Continuing with C1b, as long as I am focused on it, I see that after the four measures of A drone, comes three measures of B-flat drone, and then one measure of B-natural drone.

Thus, the bass in C1b is four measures of A drone, three measures of B-flat drone, and one measure of B-natural drone. No problem with that.

Here's my mental map of the bass in C1b:
- Four measures of A drone
- Three measures of B-flat drone
- One measure of B drone

Back to C1a

Measure six of C1a continues to drone with a D played with the A's. Measure seven of C1a continues to drone with D# played with the A, and last but not least, measure 69 of C1a drones for four notes with the E played with the A. On the last beat of the last measure of C1a, we play what looks like part of E Major as we head back to the tonic, which is A minor at the beginning of C2.

Review of Bass Parts of C1a and C1b

C1a and C1b both have eight measures. C1a bass is A drone for five measures, A drone with a D for one measure, A drone with a D# for one measure, and then a transition (modulation) measure going from A drone with E to E-G#.

C1b drones on A for four measures, drones on B-flat for three measures, and ends with one measure of B drone.

You might, at this point, want to play these bass figures to get the feel for them and to incorporate them into your tactile, visual, and auditory memory. When you are fairly familiar with what's happening in the bass, divide and conquer the treble, which will be easy if you understand the rhythm and know how to count to six.

Side Note About Auditory Memory

Some people have it, and some don't. If you have it, use it, and if you don't, don't fret about it. Ulysses S. Grant said, "I only know two tunes: one of them is Yankee Doodle, and the other isn't." Believe it or not, some people have the auditory equivalent of photographic memory, what psychologists have dubbed "phonographic memory." My wife, Ethel, can listen to the briefest excerpt of a musical piece, often for a second, and identify the title, composer, and sing it herself.

Divide and Conquer C1a

C1a measure one has one treble note, an A held for the first beat. Bingo, we now know how to play measure 62. Since this is 1/8th of C1a, we are already 12.5% ahead. (Remember, it pays to celebrate small victories.) As measure 62 and measure 70 are so similar, we may as well memorize measure 70 now by just adding a C in the treble and a low A in the bass. Bingo, we now know how to play two measures of the 16 in section C, and therefore we are 1/8th or 12.5% finished with this section.

PIANO BY HEART COMPANION

C1a measure two has only one chord in the treble, and that is held for the whole measure.

Student Patten: That chord looks strange, but it isn't hard to play. (It is one of the three diminished four-note chords in Western music.) Put your fingers on all four notes and get the feel. Note that each finger is separated from its neighbor by two semitones. Some people have called this chord C# minor 7th, but for the life of me, I can't see how that could be true. C# minor is the relative minor of E Major, so I guess this makes some sense to some people. Or, I could say that the first two notes are the bottom of E minor, and the top two notes are the top of F# Major. That is true. But who cares? In this case, it is easier to put my hands on the keys, note the position, and play it as a four-note diminished E chord, which it is—and the best chunking tool at this point. Notice the sound tends to startle us, and that may have been the effect Beethoven wanted.

After playing this diminished E chord and holding it for the full three beats of the measure, what am I going to play next? That's easy. A diminished chord resolves somewhere, and in this case, I already have a hint as to where—upward to D minor by moving my thumb to F, the second (middle) note of D minor. I move my thumb to F and index finger up to the third (end note) of D minor. That reminds me that the next chord to be played is D minor, and the simplest way to get to that chord is to use my thumb and index fingers and place my pinky on the upper D. This is D minor in first inversion and held for two beats of the measure.

BERNARD M. PATTEN

WHENCE COMES THE CHARM OF MUSIC?

❖ ❖ ❖

A case could be made for the idea that the charm of music—part of the charm anyway—stems from the tension and release that occurs when the key changes from dominant to tonic. If that is true, it would explain the major organizing principle of *Für Elise,* where A minor alternates with some form of E major. Anyway, measure two shouldn't pose much of a problem since it is so simple. And guess what? Measure two of C1b is identical, so bingo! We know four measures of section C—two in C1a and two in C1b.

On to Measure Three

Measure three starts with D minor in the first inversion. D minor is almost the subdominant of A minor. Hold D minor for two beats (four A's in the bass) and then play C#E followed by DF. C# leads into D (tell yourself), just the way E leads into F, as both C# and E are a semitone below DF. Another way to look at these is as if they are simple dichords. So play C#E and then play the next dichord up, which is DF. Play this a few times and then play the first three measures of C1a in sequence. Pretty good! Note also that the third measure of C1b is identical to the third measure of C1a. Now on to measure four of C1a.

Measure four repeats the DF that ended measure three but adds a G#. This same chord is played again on beat three (count five if you are counting to six the way I do), leading right into A minor that begins measure five and is held for the duration of the drone. Measure four of C1b is identical except the G# is omitted. But if you played it with the G#, few would notice. G# can be viewed as a lead tone to A, and Beethoven may have heard and intended it as such. Who knows?

For me, that G#DF chord is actually three notes of a G# four-note diminished chord. It sounds on beat one and beat three and leads right into A minor of measure five of C1a. Visualize the written notes in your mind's eye, keep track of the rhythm, and mastery will soon follow.

Now for the hard part of C1a, the last three measures. We already know the bass, so we just have to add the treble. The rhythm of measure six is the same as measure three, and the notes are a sequence descending one note at a time. You can even think of the descending notes as the same descending trichord that was part of part A (DCB) or of the arpeggio section of easy B (DCB) to which the FED has been added a sixth down the road. Thus, DF on beat one is held until beat three where we play CE followed by BD. This is an orderly descent of what is a familiar trichord in this piece, and the order and sequence should help us remember it. The last two measures, we shall leave to your ingenuity to memorize. Sooner or later, you have to learn how to memorize on your own. Hint: The first chord, looking at bass and treble, is a C diminished, which leads into a kind of C major that transitions to E7 to get to the first measure of C1b.

Student Patten: In fact, I get a lot of pleasure in playing these measures correctly, and I like the way it sounds when E7 leads right into the first measure of C1b. Eventually, using your memory friends—visual association, auditory association, touch association, intellectual association, emotional associations—you will play this section without much effort or conscious thought. You will play it automatically, as automatically as you tie the laces of your shoes.

Teacher Jimmy: What is your emotional association with part C? I'm curious.

Student Patten: That's easy—gloom and doom. Beethoven was having a bad hair day. Or worried about his hearing. Or unhappy his marriage proposal was refused.

We already know the first four measures of C1b because they are so similar to the first four measures of C1a. Measure five of C1b has the same rhythm as measure five of C1a, and instead of an A minor chord, the DF of D minor is sounded and held for the duration of the measure. Measure six has the same rhythm as measure six in C1a and can be viewed as a descent of some adjacent notes of the B-flat major scale—a trichord again with the sixth note below. Make sure you know where it starts. The descent starts with E-flat G and works down, ending on C-E-flat. So the note on top at the beginning is the note (E-flat) you end up on at the bottom.

Play these, and your hand and ear will get used to them. The B-flat in the bass should clue you into the fact that this measure has flats. In fact, it leads right into B-flat major in the first inversion, and that, in turn, leads into D minor on the third beat.

The last measure of C1b is unique, so you should have no trouble memorizing it. The first chord (whatever it is) is played and held for two beats, and the second (which looks like an E7) is sounded on beat 3 and held. We have already covered the bridging cadence to get to the arpeggios, and so we are pretty close to mastering section C. Review and play it as many times as you need to. Play and test yourself to see how much you do remember. Correct mistakes and fill in memory blanks as needed. If you find yourself having a particularly difficult time on a particular part, make more associations, check the score to visualize the notation, and practice, practice, practice.

Rome wasn't built in a day, and *Für Elise* won't get into your third-stage memory overnight. Be easy on yourself. 80% correct is good enough. Perfect is the enemy of the good. The real world of music performance, as opposed to the unreal world of studio learning, is very forgiving.

Tips And Tricks – What Is a Good Way of Keeping Track of Where You Are in C?

Student Patten: As mentioned, memory is aided, not hurt, by an abundance of associations. The associations that actually help me the most are counting by the numbers. Each measure of section C has six sixteenth notes in the bass, so that will be how I know where I am and what I am doing; I will just keep counting to six, just the way Homer counted to six on each line that he spoke in the hexameter of *The Iliad*. Hence, follow the score as I proceed, but remember all forms of counting are merely preliminary guides to habit. If not discarded, they may defeat their own end. Pupils, for example, who persist in counting aloud when practicing may feel lost (due to the state-dependent effect) without this mental support. During practice, if you need to, think a phrase, counting audibly; then play without counting, allowing the sense of time to guide the movements naturally. Aim for automaticity.

Doing What Comes Naturally

C1a starts with A on top and the A on the bottom. The top note is held for one beat, while the left hand plays A number two. Now keep counting out the A's in the numerical system that you learned in kindergarten: after two comes three, then six (only kidding). We were trying to see if you were still awake. After three comes four, then five, then six.

In the mind, it could look like this with the * meaning the note is held:

Measure one of C1a:
Treble: A*
(Counts) 1 2 3 4 5 6 (As in bass)
OR Bass: AAAAAA

After counting six A's, we know the next measure starts with A again, combined with the weird chord that we called the diminished and others say is C# 7th. What it really is doesn't matter because we know exactly where our right hand should be to play the E-G-B-flat-C#.

Since this is measure two, hold the right hand chord and continue to count out the six A's while dropping on them—2,3,4,5,6. When you hit 6, you should be reminded that a new measure is starting—measure 3.

Possible mental map of Measure two of C1a:
Treble: Weird Chord (diminished as discussed)
(Counts) 1 2 3 4 5 6
Bass: AAAAAA

Measure three (conveniently) has three treble sounds at the first A, the fifth A, and the sixth A in the bass. The first inversion D minor is held until count five when we will play the notes D#E (with bass A note five), leading into the DF (also a part of D minor) in treble. DF sounds with A6, so we know that we have finished with measure three and must sound measure four.

If need be, you can make a mental map of Measure three of C1a.

PIANO BY HEART COMPANION

Measure Four

Measure 4 starts with the DF sounded at the end of measure three with a G# added. Meanwhile, keep counting A's in the bass 1, 2, 3, 4, and on 5 (beat 3 of the measure), hit the same chord again and hold until A6 is over. The memory of measure four is helped by recalling that measure three is the present peak of sounding in treble with three sounding, and thereafter, it is down to two sounding in measure four, headed to one sounding (the tonic) in measure five. Magic measure five has the A minor tonic held for the whole measure while the drone continues in bass, 1, 2, 3, 4, 5, 6.

That measure five, with its easy A minor and A drone, reminds us that the descent must start in measure 6, and my pinky on the left hand must help facilitate the descent by playing the D with A. The rhythm is familiar—a hit on A1, 5, and 6—and the descent is by whole notes in an interval of a sixth. But where to start? Aye, there's the question. Answer: top note and bottom note are both D, so the sequence will be DF, CE, BD. OK, great. This descent is the trichord of part A theme two of *Für Elise*, so that association may help us remember where to start.

Hang in there! Only two measures to go, and they are hard. Not only are they hard, but they sound like the descent into hell. D in bass moves up to D#, and the right hand plays CA with an F# as the middle tone. On note 5 of the bass, this same combo is played again without the F#. And then the pinky moves up again in the bass to E, and the right hand plays that CA again (beat one), EC (beat two), and then DB (beat three). For beat three, my index moves down to G#, and we head into the first measure of C2.

It might be helpful for you to do the same sort of analysis for C1b that we did for C1a and, through the technique of narrative and intellectual analysis, organize your approach to C1b.

Student Patten: For me, the idea of counting to six in C1b works well, and I just have to keep in mind that C1b differs from C1a at measure four and that at measure five, B-flat takes over in the bass for three measures, finally arriving at a special measure eight with B-natural in the bass and those unique chords in treble on beat one and three (bass notes one and five).

MEMORIZING MUSIC IS HARD WORK

◆◆◆

Remember, memorizing music is hard work. Concentrate on what you are doing, and don't get distracted. Handle small chunks little by little of each part until you have them pretty much in the memory, and then go on. Brain, fingers, eyes, and ears must all work together on the task. Approach the music as a whole—how it sounds, looks on the page, feels on the keys, and so forth—but focus intensively on one thing at a time. Work as slowly or as fast as the music requires. Some sections will come easy, others hard. That's normal and expected. Play exactly what is on the score—correct rhythms, notes, and all the other details. Don't make the mistake of just learning notes at first. You might learn the wrong rhythm or phrasing or dynamics and then have trouble correcting what you have memorized. It is difficult to unlearn something once it has passed into your stage-three memory. Use some of the historical information that you learned to help you make associations to help you remember. The opening melody of, say, a Chopin E-flat Nocturne is straight out of Italian opera. To play it as if you didn't know that is to miss a point. Bach combines German organization with Lutheran spirituality and well-established European musical styles, particularly the Italian style and sometimes the French style. If you don't believe what we just said about Bach, listen to the *Coffee Cantata*.

Memorize Without Distraction

Set up a reasonable timetable for memorization and stick to it without interruptions or distractions. When you can play the entire piece ten times without significant errors, you are OK. Remember that memory needs constant renewal, so don't be discouraged if tomorrow you make some mistakes or have hesitations. Those mistakes or hesitations are important. They are telling you that those parts of the piece need more attention and more work. Also, don't be surprised if you wake up the next day and suddenly the part of the piece that gave you trouble is now a piece of (chocolate) cake.

Tips and Tricks

OK, great. You have fair control of the two most difficult parts (B and C) of *Für Elise*. Don't let them slip out of your memory. Play them anytime you can and play them multiple times a day. Sooner or later, you won't have to think too much about them, and you will have reached the stage of AUTOMATICITY, where you will play them almost automatically, so automatically that you will be able to put your own style and feeling into the performance. And if you look at the score, it will seem to be a map of a foreign country that you once studied about in school and have now forgotten.

"Für Elise"

Bagatelle in A minor WoO 59

Ludwig van Beethoven
1770 - 1827

Then the whole thing repeats exactly starting just as it started in the beginning with ED# and working through until at the second repetition. When you get to that D and the famous trichord descent to A you know another major section is starting, namely theme two. Theme two starts with the trichord ascent of BCD ending on E, which is sounded with the C in the bass.

Theme two:

Bass then follows a very logical structure, which you should be able to figure out. Hint: try looking at the section as based on trichord descents associated with various related chords in the bass. Ascending trichord CDE matches up with CGC in base (C Major). Descending FED matches up with GGB in bass (G Major). Descending EDC matches with A minor, and last but not least, DCB matches with E with the B (the end note of the E major chord) sounded with the E in the base.

How Do We Get Out of the Bass-Ment?

Wait a second! We are way down there in the low tones. How do we get out?

The outlook isn't brilliant for it looks like we are boxed in way down in the bass. Nope, not Beethoven. He's not boxed in. No sir! Beethoven just starts jumping E's to the top and starts the ED# over again. You do the same and have fun jumping, just as Beethoven must have had fun. If you are not having fun playing the piano, what's the point?

Jumping E's outlined in red.

STYLE AND INTERPRETATION

❖ ❖ ❖

Here's how Liszt put it: "(the musician) is not a mason who, chisel in hand, faithfully and consciously whittles stone after the design of an architect. His is not the passive tool reproducing feeling and thought and adding nothing of himself. ... He is called upon to make emotion speak, and weep, and sing, and sigh – to bring it to life in his consciousness. He creates as the composer himself created, for he himself must live the passions that he will call to light in all their brilliance. He breathes life into the lethargic body, infuses it with fire..." (quoted in Friedheim, *Liszt and Life: The Recollections of a Concert Pianist*, New York, Taplinger, 1961).

Like Liszt, Paganini believed that musical notation was simply inadequate to render music. Paganini's famous declaration: "The concert is – myself."

Student Patten: The concert is myself. That's an important idea to keep in mind. It is a little grandiose, of course, but probably true. And it probably applies to your own concerts at home or elsewhere. The statement reminds me of the French Sun King (Louis XIV), who famously remarked, "L'Etat, c'est moi." "I am the state." Face it. Many people have gigantic egos.

The Score Is Not the Talmud or the Mishnah

A score (say they – Liszt and Paganini) is, at best, a rough guide to what a performer should do.

Teacher White and Student Patten: We agree. Music should come first as a form of expressed feeling and thought produced on the spot by the performer because the transcription of musical ideas from mind to paper is only approximate. That is the reason why there are so many interpretations of a given work, often as many interpretations as there are interpreters—just as there are as many types of marriage as there are couples and as many types of love as there are hearts.

Student Patten: I won't name names, but I know composers themselves, even the most accomplished, veer from the text of their own composition—playing faster or slower than indicated, stricter or more freely, even changing the indicated dynamic markings. The composer Irving Berlin (*White Christmas, God Bless America*) was famously even unable to play his own songs.

What About MM?

MM does not stand for some now-dead Hollywood goddess, Marilyn Monroe. MM stands for metronome marks. MM doesn't help much except in practice. The only precise tempo marking, according to composer Ned Rorem, is *presto possibile*. The vaguest is *con moto* (seen on many copies of *Für Elise*). Therefore, we performers have leave to change things. Yes, we can change things, and we will change things. Music as an art shows some of the primary signs of life: change and movement.

Teacher White: MM actually stands for Maelzel's Metronome. Maelzel was the man who patented the invention of the metronome in the early 1800s. Beethoven was the first notable composer to include MM markings. A note to the teachers who torture their students and kill all musical expression with the overuse of this device: Beethoven said the metronome should only be used for the first few measures and then turned off, as it destroys all life in the music. This sentiment is echoed by Liszt, Brahms, Wagner, Berlioz, Rubinstein, Gershwin, Paderewski, and Debussy. Other notables would probably agree, but I have not yet run across the quote to prove it. So, get your tempo, and then turn that thing off and let the music live.

Meanwhile, Da Vinci's static product, the *Mona Lisa*, smiles on, unchanged and unchangeable through the centuries. Thank goodness we pianists have an art that can adapt to the present circumstances, to our times, to our human feelings, and, by the way, even to the feelings, needs, and expectations of different audiences.

Student Patten: Good point. I actually try to match what I play to the audiences involved. I play a different repertoire in cocktail lounges compared to recitals in retirement homes. And a very different set of pieces before family at Thanksgiving and, of course, very different ones at Christmas time. Be prepared for different settings, and you will be better loved.

Where Do You Stand?

How about you? What's your take? How do you feel about all this? Do you stand with Liszt? Is that what you feel? Or do your ideas match up with Robert Schumann, who felt the opposite and appended to his *Album for the Young*, opus 68, this advice: "As you grow older, converse more frequently with the score than with virtuosos!"

Finish Up by Adding Part A of *Für Elise* to Parts B and C

While you are reviewing parts B and C at every opportunity, at your leisure, add part A, which has nice, easy repetitive patterns of chromatic E-D# and A minor and E Major arpeggios, along with some nice leaps in theme 2 of A from one E to another up the keyboard. Keep the organization of part A clearly in mind so that you get things straight.

Student Patten: It took me only about an hour to memorize part A and play it from memory. It is well organized and lends itself well to chunking. The haunting melody is unforgettable, so it will be very hard to get lost in part A as long as you keep track of where you are in the piece at all times. For some audiences, part A is sufficient, and it's all they want. For others, give them the whole shebang.

PIANO BY HEART COMPANION

PUTTING IT ALL TOGETHER

❖ ❖ ❖

After you have mastered part A (the part that most people love to play), put the whole piece together. Watch yourself on video and improve whatever you can. Follow your video performance with the score to ensure you don't omit any important parts.

Student Patten: My experience has been shock (and awe) when I saw the first playback and discovered that I had completely omitted part B! Now I watch myself very carefully, paying special attention to part B, making sure I get through it. Often, I silently give a sigh of relief when I reach B easy because I know from then on, it is downhill. Musical attention is often dual in character: listening to what you are playing and thinking ahead. In omitting part B, I was doing neither.

Take a short break and then come back for an equally exhaustive analysis of how to memorize a minuet by Mozart.

Only kidding.

You now have the memory tools to work on what you want to play from memory, whether it's a *Minuet in F* by Mozart, *Stormy Weather* by Arden, or anything else reasonable. It's your choice.

Good luck and happy playing.

Coda

Let us know how you made out. And let us know if you discovered any tips or tricks on your own. Dr. Patten's email is Dadpatten@aol.com; Dr. White's email is Thepianoguy@att.net.

By the way—congratulations for getting through *Für Elise* and for getting through this book. Remember to think hard until the necessary habits are trained.

This above all, a parting piece of advice for you to keep in your memory:

Have fun.

PIANO BY HEART COMPANION

BIBLIOGRAPHY

◆ ◆ ◆

Books That Might Help You with Music Memory

Aristotle on Memory, Second Edition. Sorabji, Richard. University of Chicago Press, 1972, Chicago. Much of what is here will sound quite modern even though it is over 2500 years old. Listen to the master explain how to recall something forgotten: Find a starting point that leads to the item one wishes to recollect. Start in one's thoughts from something similar, opposite, or neighboring to the thing one wishes to recollect. If someone wishes to recollect what he did last Tuesday, he may start in his thoughts from what he did Monday, which is neighboring. Then, with any luck, the image corresponding to this thing will come next to, overlap with, or even be the same as the image of the thing to be recollected. Notice how brilliantly Aristotle emphasizes the all-important point of having a starting point. Indeed, the official title of this book is often written: *Aristotle's On Memory and Reminding Oneself.*

Playing the Piano for Pleasure. Cooke, Charles. Simon & Schuster, New York, 1960. This is, of course, a classic that cannot fail to be of use to anyone who likes to play the piano. Some of the advice is dated, and some of it is emblematic of a bygone era: for instance, on page 89, the author advised, in a page break, that this would be a good place for the reader and the author to smoke a cigarette! The exact quote: "The above space indicates a pause during which author and reader will smoke a cigarette." Currently, we are sure smoking is bad for health.

BERNARD M. PATTEN

The Memory Advantage: Improve Your Memory, Mood, and Confidence Throughout Life. Crook, Thomas H. SelectBooks, Inc., New York, 2006. Lots of interesting ideas about memory and general health, some kind of hokey, but still interesting. The parts about associations and recall are standard and will be a review for anyone who has read Patten on music memory.

Memorizing Music. Cumberland, Gerald. The Richards Press, London, 1923. Highly recommended, a source of many insights into the nature of memory and the methods of memorizing music.

The Essence of Music. Busoni, Ferruccio. Rockliff Publishing Corporation, 1957. Vastly overrated, this book reminds me of blarney, lots of talk but very little meaning. The word "blarney" derives from the Earl of Blarney, the sixteenth-century Irish chief who, like the other chiefs, was required to affirm allegiance to the British crown and to Queen Elizabeth I. The Earl gave such a long florid speech that nobody could tell whether he was for submission or rebellion. If after reading Busoni, you can tell what he thinks is the essence of music, then please let me know because I could not make head or tail of his position on the subject. His was first-class Blarney.

The Lives of the Piano. Gaines, James R. Hilltown Press, republished by Holt, Rinehart, and Winston, New York, 1981. Eight essays about the love of people for their pianos with lots of insight and wonderful anecdotes. Anthony Burgess (the very same literary man of fame) does an excellent job of reviewing from his Irish perspective the piano's social and intellectual history. The most personal and, therefore, the most revealing essay is that by composer Ned Rorem, who admits that he has difficulty playing his own compositions and even more difficulty memorizing them.

Guide to Memorizing Music. Goodrich, A.J. The John Church Company, New York, 1906. Dated and quaint, but interesting because of the way that the author wars against memory of music by rote. He understands the need to chunk and the need to understand the overall design of music. The best use of this book is to go over each music example and follow along with the author to see how he would understand and then memorize the piece.

How to Play Piano: Everything You Need to Know to Play the Piano. Evans, Roger. St. Martin's Press, 1981. Despite the false presumption behind the title (the book doesn't have everything you need to play the piano—how could it?), this little book has plenty of information on how to play the piano. The chapter on *Playing to an Audience* has lots of sound advice. Most of the book is basic and might be a good place to start if you are just beginning your piano fun.

In Search of Memory: The Emergence of a New Science of Mind. Kandel, Eric R. Detailed autobiography of the man who made modern memory science and who won the Nobel Prize in Medicine for his work. The mechanisms of memory are illustrated clearly and correctly. Memory science is complicated, and his is the simplest (yet complex) way of explaining it.

Music by Heart. Mackinnon, Lilias. Greenwood Press, Connecticut, 1926. If you have time for only one book on music memory, read this one. It is compendious, perhaps too compendious because the author covers the smallest detail about music and memory. The use of color associations for memorization of scores is particularly interesting, as is the use of arrows as reminder pegs. But those who over-mark their music may end by remembering the marks instead of the music. Mark up your music copy, but don't mark it up too much.

BERNARD M. PATTEN

Beethoven FÜR ELISE. Miller, Neil. Analyzed Editions, 2007. This looks self-published. It is heavy on intellectual analysis and light on memory techniques, but nevertheless filled with wisdom and good advice. The second part of the pamphlet is taken from one of his other books and goes over basic music theory, including the cycle of fifths.

The Seven Sins of Memory: How the Mind Forgets and Remembers. Schacter, Daniel L. Houghton Mifflin Company, New York, 2001. A great work by one of the world's memory experts. Particularly interesting are the studies of memory falsification and retrospective fitting, miscues, transience, blocking, misattribution, bias, suggestibility, and persistence. He is a little weak on the neurology of memory, but who cares?

Wax Tablets of the Mind: Cognitive Studies of Memory and Literacy in Classical Antiquity. Small, Jocelyn Penny. Routledge, New York, 1997. A major scholarly work that explores the relationship between literacy and memory in classical antiquity from the point of view of modern psychology. Dr. Small is a classical archaeologist who views memory from multiple cultural perspectives. A cross-cultural study of memory (for instance) of the author found that one's cultural expectations may affect the accuracy of one's memory. (Really? HO HO HO). If you grow up being told that your memory will get worse as you get older, it will. Conversely, if you are Chinese and believe that being old is not something negative, but something positive, then your memory will remain strong. Particularly valuable are the chapters discussing the techniques that our ancient ancestors used to memorize what they needed to know. Such techniques are not without modern application, but the detail that the ancients used for their mental images seems excessive. In medieval mnemonic systems, the relative sizes of the images are adjusted to make room for items to stand out better, crowding is discouraged, items are erased by prescribed standards, fog and smoke are avoided in the image, and an image lamp can be brought up to illuminate what is obscure. Items may come to be noticed or cease to be noticed in predictable sequences and checkable ways, as the background color changes or contrast is increased or reduced. Sometimes the ancient images get out of control as, for instance, in *Rhetorica ad Herennium*, where we are advised to use an image of testicles to represent the witnesses (testes) in a lawsuit.

An Actor Prepares. Stanislovski, Constantin. Routledge, New York and London, 2003. A classic. Acting and piano recital share many features, including techniques on how to avoid stage fright, how to memorize, and how to put human emotion into the performance. In acting, as in playing music, the emotion part is important. Otherwise, the performance will be flat, dull, and boring.

Neurobic Exercises to Help Prevent Memory Loss and Increase Mental Fitness

Keep Your Brain Alive. Lawrence C. Katz, Ph.D., & Manning Rubin. Workman Publishing Company, New York, 1999. Excellent. Do the work and benefit your brain.

Train Your Mind, CHANGE YOUR BRAIN. Sharon Begley. Sometimes dull and hokey, sometimes interesting. Hits most of the important points about augmenting mental function but has a definite bias in favor of the Buddhist contemplative tradition. There are errors about human neuroanatomy, particularly about the central nervous connections in the visual system, but for a popular work, it is not bad.

How to Read a Poem. Burton Raffel. New American Library, 1984. A good place to start if you want to know how to recite and understand poetry. Some of the interpretations are off but interesting. The poems themselves are worth memorizing. The great American composer MacDowell considered himself and every other great composer "tone poets." Student Patten, having been trained to copy the greats, now considers himself, whenever he plays the piano, a tone poet. This is not a bad attitude for any pianist interested in making emotionally touching and expressive music.

How to Think Like Leonardo da Vinci. Michael J. Gelb. Dell Trade Paperback, 1998. Fun and funny with some nice exercises and some food for thought on how to improve your life, wealth, thinking, memory, and outlook. It's OK to think like the master (Leonardo), but please try to finish more of the tasks you start than he did. Carry-on and carry-through are, as every pianist knows, as important as starting. Leonardo, as everyone knows, was deficient in the extreme in both carry-on and carry-through.

Dumbth. Steve Allen. Prometheus Books, 1998. Much of this is about thinking clearly and productively, but it also covers 101 ways to improve your mental effectiveness. The beginning of the book is off-putting because Steve sounds like the intellectual snob that he is. Most people are put off by snobs. Don't be a snob.

How to Be Twice as Smart. Scott Witt. Rewards Books, 2002. Excellent in every way. Highly recommended. This may have been self-published, but it is firmly based and well-written. If you get and read only one exercise book, this is the one to get. It is not titled correctly, however. The real title should have been: *How to Look Four to Ten Times Smarter Than You Are*.

Building Mental Muscle. David Gamon, Ph.D., and Allen D. Bragdon. 1998. Excellent collection of exercises for the right and left sides of your brain. Other books by the same authors are also worth a look: *Building Left Brain Power, Exercises for the Whole Brain, Right-Brain Teasers*.

Older and Wiser. Richard M. Restak, M.D. Berkley Books, 1997. A neurologist tells how to maintain mental ability for as long as you live. Upbeat and reassuring, but also grounded in neuroscience with 30 practical suggestions on how to maximize mental performance. Probably directed more to seniors than to youth.

Mental Dynamics: Power Thinking for Personal Success. K. Thomas Finley. Prentice-Hall, 1966. Use this if you wish to raise a genius child.

Mozart's Brain and the Fighter Pilot: Unleashing Your Brain's Potential. Richard Restak, M.D. Three Rivers Press, 2001. Really cool book. See also his book mentioned above.

Put on a Happy Face. Cooper Edens and Richard Kehl. Chronicle Books, 2003. Studies show that the more you smile, the happier you feel and are. In this book, you will see what a good smile and a happy face should look like. For reasons discussed, try to smile during your piano performances no matter what. The audience wants to see happy, smiling performers. When you smile, you get happy, and your audience gets happy too. Anything wrong with that?

Games for the Superintelligent. James F. Fixx. Galahad Books, 1998. Math, Logic, and Word Puzzles from Mensa. Worth a look, but don't get discouraged if you can't do most of the problems. Studies have shown you don't have to do much mental exercise to stay mentally fit. Just a little will do. The ACTIVE study (a scientific study of seniors designed to see what items correlate with memory function) proved that minimal memory training and logic training have measurable beneficial effects ten years later without any training in the interim. Studies also show TV is bad for the brain. Do not watch it.

The Mature Mind: The Positive Power of the Aging Brain. Gene D. Cohen, M.D., Ph.D. Basic Books, 2005. Getting old isn't for sissies, and old dogs can prove that point by learning new tricks. The author (Cohen) has a gigantic ego, which sometimes gets in the way of the facts. He has been the director of the National Institutes of Aging and knows his stuff. Some unfortunate misquotes (particularly of modern poetry) crept into the manuscript, proving once again that when an expert steps out of his field, he might get into trouble. The references to the literature and the internet resources are worth the price of this book many times over.

Memory Augmentation, Mnemonics, and Memory Exercises

The Harvard Medical School Guide to Achieving Optimal Memory, Aaron P. Nelson with Susan Gilbert, McGraw-Hill, 2005. Although obviously written down and dumbed down for general readership consumption (I almost wrote sales), this book has several redeeming features, among which are self-appraisals and tests of your memory to see if you are actually normal or have a problem that requires professional help. Skip the discussions of neurological diseases, as they are simple and simplistic. Some of the so-called medical advice is just wrong. For instance, there is no general health benefit to taking Vitamin E. In fact, (recent large-scale scientific studies show that) vitamin E will tend to make you sick, give you hemorrhages, and promote heart failure and hospitalization. Vitamin E does not prevent cancer, stroke, heart disease, and so forth. The United States government spent millions proving that taking vitamin E is a bad idea for most people.

PIANO BY HEART COMPANION

Your Memory: A User's Guide, Alan Baddeley, Macmillan Publishing, 1982.

The Memory Prescription: Dr. Gary Small's 14-Day Plan to Keep Your Brain and Body Young, Hyperion, New York, 2004. (Note: some interesting ideas and some good exercises, but also some stuff (especially about diet) that is just silly.)

Memory Makes Money, Harry Lorayne, Little, Brown. All of Harry's books are essentially the same*: How to Develop a Super-Power Memory, Secrets of Memory, Instant Mind Power, Memory Isometrics* (this is the one Dr. Patten trained on), *Good Memory – Good Student!, The Memory Book* (this one sold over 2 million copies), *The Page-A-Minute Memory Book, Remembering People*. The books are the same, but the titles are different. My recommendation: Get one of Harry's books. Read it through. Use the parts you need; forget the rest. And if you want a good laugh, get Harry's book *Super Memory Super Student: How to Raise Your Grades in 30* Days. Turn to page 124, Chapter 18 on music memory. Harry is all at sea making up complicated mnemonics to memorize how to read key signatures. What a waste of time! And note this: Here's how he memorizes the components of the D major chord: "A dean holds half a knife and fights an ape." Where (we guess) Dean reminds us of D, half (we guess) is supposed to remind us of F as the word half ends in the letter F, and the knife reminds us that F is sharp and leads to an A (the ape). Aren't you glad you learned the diatonic scale (whole step, whole step, half step, whole step, whole step, whole step, half step) and can instantly play any major chord without thinking much about it? See if you roll off your chair on this: Harry memorizes the position of the keys on the piano:

"All the G and A keys
Are between the black threes
And 'tween the twos are all the D'd

Then on the right side of the threes
Will be found the B's and C's
But on the left side of the threes
Are all the F's and all the E's."

Truly ridiculous, right? Harry evidently didn't get that the keys are organized in the exact sequence of the letters of the alphabet, and all you had to know is where any one key was and you could easily deduce where the others lay. Those of you who have finished reading this book automatically know where any key is located. The automaticity in performance is fundamental to superior achievement. Thank the gods that the sequence of keys is ABCDEFG. If you know where middle C is (it's right under the manufacturer's name on the piano), every other key follows logically. ABCDEFG — that sequence is easier to recall than the complicated mnemonic proposed by Harry Lorayne, an illustration that the proper recognition of important patterns is worth ten thousand mnemonics.

Reversing Memory Loss, Vernon H. Mark, M.D., with Jeffrey P. Mark, M.Sc., Houghton Mifflin Company, 1999. Some good advice from a geriatric and psychiatry point of view based on decades of experience and know-how, but a little simple and simplistic.

The Memory Workbook, Douglas J. Mason, Psy.D., and Michael L. Kohl, Psy.D., New Harbinger Publications, 2001. Techniques to exercise your brain and improve your memory. Some of the material on dementia is now dated. If you ever get through all of the exercises in this book, you will be a memory genius.

Total Memory Workout, Cynthia R. Green, Ph.D., Bantam, 2001. Based on her experience in the memory enhancement program at Mount Sinai Hospital, she offers eight easy steps to maximum memory fitness. She has some good, simple tips, but for the most part, a lot of it is already known to you because you read this book by Doctor Patten.

How to Remember, Bruno Furst, Greenberg Publisher, 1947. Lotte Furst (his wife) probably did most of the work for this book, but her name is nowhere in sight. This was one of the classics by two (Lotte and Bruno Furst) of the greatest American mnemonists of all time.

General Interest

King of Ragtime: Scott Joplin and His Era, Edward A. Berlin, Oxford University Press, New York, 1994. By far the best book on the subject. The crush event and the music Joplin produced because of it are discussed in detail. If you wish to know how program music is put together and the narrative forms that will help you remember the music, then take a look at this classic work on Joplin.

Views & Reviews: The History of Memory Arts, Bernard M. Patten, MD, FACP, *Neurology* 1990;40:346-352. By far and away the best succinct survey of memory arts. Ancient humans, lacking devices to store large amounts of information, invented and developed a system of mnemonics, which evolved and passed to modern times. The mnemonics, collectively known as the *Ancient Art of Memory*, were discovered in 447 BC by a Greek poet, Simonides, and were adequately described by Cicero, Quintilian, and Pliny. These arts fell into neglect after Alaric sacked Rome in 410 AD but were subsequently revived in 1323 by Saint Thomas Aquinas, who transferred them from a division of rhetoric to ethics and used them to recall Catholic doctrines and versions of biblical history. In 1540, Saint Ignatius Loyola used mnemonic images to affirm the faith with his newly formed Society of Jesus and tried to convert the Ming dynasty in China by teaching these memory skills to Chinese nobles. Today, the ancient memory arts have applications in pilot training, gambling, mentalism, and telepathy demonstrations and may have a role in the rehabilitation of brain-damaged patients. Objective testing confirms that with the use of these memory skills, recall is increased at least 10-fold, and the memory deficits of proactive and retroactive inhibition do not exist.

The Medieval Craft of Memory: An Anthology of Texts and Pictures, Mary Carruthers and Jan M. Ziolkowski, eds., University of Pennsylvania Press, Philadelphia, 2002. Take a look at this to see the kinds of images used by your ancestors to remember all sorts of complex information. The medieval arts of memory cannot be learned by generalized rules alone but require the active use of an individual's imagination. The subject matter was mainly religious. For instance, the image of penance as a seraph is quite imposing when seen as a whole, but because it is easily understood through the memorization of its thirty logically placed visual components, penance becomes a very livable and humane sort of doctrine, indispensable to any twelfth-century reader striving for holiness to avoid the eternal punishment of Hell.

Medieval Music and the Art of Memory, Anna Maria Busse Berger, University of California Press, Berkeley, 2005. Excellent exposition of memory as a craft with heavy emphasis on images as mnemonics. The text explains how such images were used to memorize music and as tools for making musical thoughts. The complexity of images used to memorize music is daunting. Obviously, medieval musicians were highly motivated and felt empowered now that they had a written text, which was (and often still is) essential for encoding music correctly.

Ancient & Medieval Memories: Studies in the Reconstruction of the Past, Janet Coleman, Cambridge

University Press, 1992, New York. This scholarly work is also a labor of love and is chock-full of details on how our ancient ancestors remembered things. Covered in detail are the memory ideas and systems of Plato, Aristotle, Cicero (particularly important), Pliny, Plotinus, Augustine, Benedict, Bede, St. Bernard, Abelard, Dun Scotus, William of Ockham, and others. The book concludes with an all too brief account of the modern theories of mind and remembering.

Brain Tricks, David L. Weiner, Prometheus Books, 1995. Why the brain makes mistakes and how to cope with our defective brains.

The Brain Has a Mind of Its Own, Richard Restak, M.D., Harmony Books, 1991. That is the problem, of course. The brain does have a mind of its own, and we must keep it in line and disciplined by consciously controlling it. The brain doesn't even know many times when it is making mistakes or believing nonsense, so we have to learn to control the brain and check and recheck its work products.

Influence: The Psychology of Persuasion, Robert B. Cialdini, Ph.D., William Morrow. Too bad this book is mainly read by the wrong people. It was designed to shield you from irrational influences and has been a popular read for advertising execs and marketers. Over 500,000 copies sold. Some of the six major influences are covered. Read this and weep. Almost every advertisement and every business involves deception. The deception succeeds because of the defects in the human brain, which functions as a coincidence machine, connecting, for instance, a beautiful woman with a certain brand of cigarette just because the two are pictured together. The connection, of course, is completely irrational. Smoking that brand of cigarette will not make you young or beautiful. In fact, the opposite is true. Smoking will wrinkle facial skin and make you look older than you are, not younger. This kind of advertisement is now illegal, and for good reason. It was an ad for Virginia Slims cigarettes.

Brain, Mind, and Behavior, Floyd E. Bloom and Arlyne Lazerson, W.H. Freeman and Company, 1988. Scientifically sound but not for the faint-hearted. Most normal people will be adrift after page one. Scientists can understand this book and benefit from it.

The Making of Memory, Steven Rose, Anchor Books, 1992. Many pages of text and illustrations have been lifted directly from Dr. Patten's scientific papers. Dr. Patten did not sue because Dr. Patten is a nice guy, and Dr. Rose did reference Dr. Patten's work in the bibliography.

The Memory Palace of Matteo Ricci, Jonathan D. Spence, Viking, 1984. (Note: This is a scholarly demonstration of mnemonic techniques from the history of the Jesuits in China.) Most of the techniques used will be familiar after you have finished reading Patten on music memory.

The Art of Memory, Frances A. Yates, The University of Chicago Press, 1966. The best scholarly work on the ancient art of memory and, by extrapolation, its modern applications. Dr. Patten has read this three times and got more out of it each time. A classic that has earned its position on the Modern Library's 100 best nonfiction books of the twentieth century.

Creative Thinking

A Whack on the Side of the Head, Roger von Oech, Ph.D., Warner Books, 1983. How to unlock your brain for innovation. The tips are worth the price, and so is the bibliography.

Serendipity – Accidental Discoveries in Science, Royston M. Roberts, John Wiley & Sons, Inc., 1989. Chance favors the prepared mind.

Conceptual Blockbusting: A Guide to Better Ideas, James L. Adams, W.W. Norton, 1979.

The Art of Persuasion, Linda Bridges & William F. Rickenbacker, National Review, 1991. Use this as your guide if you really want to be a pro at persuasion.

Put Your Mother on the Ceiling, Richard de Mille, Viking Compass, 1973. Originally intended for children, the games in imaginative thinking work also for adults. They suggest putting your mother on the ceiling is good practice if you wish to develop your visual memory skills. Dr. Patten, as you may recall, used a Coke bottle for visual memory training. De Mille uses mothers.

Last but Not Least

Highly recommended: Dr. Patten's masterpiece of erudition: *Making Mental Might: How to Look Ten Times Smarter than You Are*, Bernard M. Patten, AB, MD, FACP, FRSM, FTNS, FAAN, Identity Publications, 2021. The very best (according to Patten) clearly written book discussing in detail the neurology of learning and memory with major examples and detailed techniques for improving mental might.

www.ingramcontent.com/pod-product-compliance
Lightning Source LLC
LaVergne TN
LVHW012249070526
838201LV00107B/308/J